21 Easy Ukulele Songs for Christmas

BEGINNING UKULELE SONGS BOOK 7

FOR SOPRANO, CONCERT, AND TENOR UKULELES WITH C TUNING (G, C, E, A)

Rebecca Bogart and Jenny Peters

LARGE PRINT EDITION

(PREVIOUSLY PUBLISHED ISBN 978-1-5186815-5-4)

This book includes a free online video course.

To see a sample video visit

ukulele.io/XmasVideo

Ordering Information:
Quantity sales. Special discounts are available on quantity purchases by corporations, associations, and others. For details, contact the "Special Sales Department" at the address above.

21 Easy Ukulele Songs for Christmas /Rebecca Bogart and Jenny Peters —Large Print Edition
ISBN 979-8-9877066-0-2

Contents

Do You Want to Play Easy Ukulele Christmas Music Now?

Learning holiday music doesn't have to be frustrating when you learn with *21 Easy Ukulele Songs for Christmas.* We've written it specifically for beginning ukulele players who have learned the C, F, and G7 chords and a few basic strums. And we've put careful thought into creating great-sounding yet easy-to-play versions of seasonal favorites. We've arranged the book so you can master the easiest music first and then gradually tackle harder tunes as your skills improve.

With *21 Easy Ukulele Songs for Christmas,* you'll be excited to pick up your ukulele and tackle the new music of the season! And soon you'll find it easy to strike up an impromptu caroling session when you take out your uke and start to strum – even with people who wouldn't be caught singing at any other time of the year! You'll be able to relax, celebrate and share the joy of Christmas music with your family and friends.

What Songs Are Included?

You'll find a nice mix of secular and sacred tunes in this book, with a bit of history and some little-known facts for each one:

- Oh Christmas Tree
- I Saw Three Ships
- Jingle Bells
- Good King Wenceslas
- Up on the Housetop
- Over the River and Through the Wood
- Come, Little Children
- Away in a Manger
- Silent Night
- Joy to the World
- Jolly Old Saint Nicholas
- Auld Lang Syne
- Deck the Halls
- Patapan
- God Rest Ye Merry Gentlemen
- We Three Kings
- What Child Is This?
- Come All Ye Faithful
- Hark the Herald Angels Sing
- The Twelve Days of Christmas
- We Wish You a Merry Christmas

Lots of Ways to Play Each Song

You can either sing the song and strum the chords or you can play the melody. All of the songs are written out on a standard music staff with a treble clef. Lyrics appear below the musical notation, and a chord letter appears above it each time there's a chord change. If you play by ear, the lyrics and chord changes are all you need. If you read music, you can learn the melody and rhythm from the standard music notation.

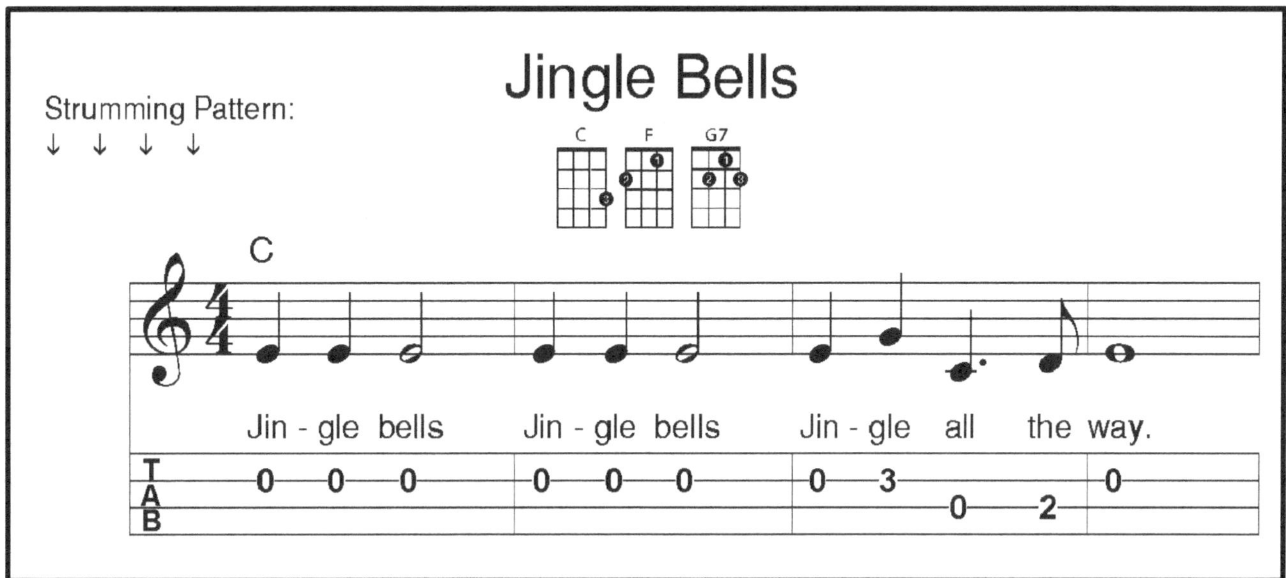

If you have a friend or family member who plays ukulele, you can create duets, with one person playing melody and the other one strumming chords. That's because below the music staff is a tab staff that works like a road map showing you how to pluck the melody on the strings of the ukulele.

We usually suggest several strumming patterns for each song. Some strums are easier when you are first learning a song, and some are more difficult so you can upgrade to a more complicated rhythm as you gain more skill.

Includes Free Online Video Course

Each song has an accompanying online lesson video with lyrics and chord changes so you can hear as well as see the music. It's a very fun and friendly way to learn musical skills. To set up your account on our website, please follow the directions in the section at the end of the book called "How to Access Your Free Video Course at ukulele.io."

About This Book

Welcome to 21 *Easy Ukulele Songs for Christmas!* We're glad you're here. Before we get started: if you see a word in ***bold italics***, that means it's a musical term defined in a glossary we keep updated at ukulele.io/glossary. There is also a chord glossary at the end of the book with photographs of the left hand shape plus the chord stamp for the most common ukulele chords.

Don't Miss Out on Your Free Video Course!

Hey, we just wanted to remind you that you get a free video course with purchase of this book. The videos can help answer questions you might not even know you had. They also make learning ukulele easier and more fun. You'll see exactly how to place your hands to do the strums and make the chords. You'll be able to hear exactly how the chords and strums should sound. And if you don't know one of the songs or if you don't read music, the videos will help you hear how the songs go.

Each chapter of the book has its own matching unit in the video course. In the back of the book is a section with step-by-step instructions and screenshots to show you how to access your free course at our website, ukulele.io. Or you can visit ukulele.io/access-free-video-course.

In the free video course, we perform simple duet versions of each tune. Here's what we do:

1. Sing and strum one or two verses

2. Jenny plays the melody and Rebecca strums the chords

3. Sing and strum another verse and/or chorus to round out the song.

Use your own imagination and preferences to come up with a way that works best for you.

Some Notes on Strumming

Here are the three main strumming patterns we will refer to in this book.

Strum #1 All down strums on a steady ***beat***.

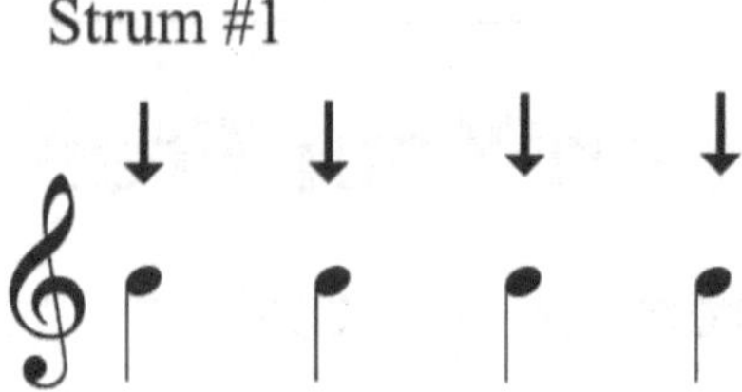

Strum #2 Down-up strums with an even division of the beat. All the strums are equally spaced.

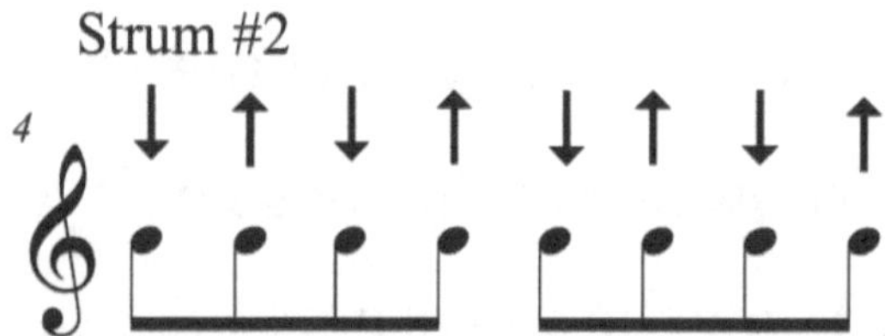

Strum #3 Down-up strums with an uneven division of the beat. Wait a little longer after each down strum before you play the next up strum.

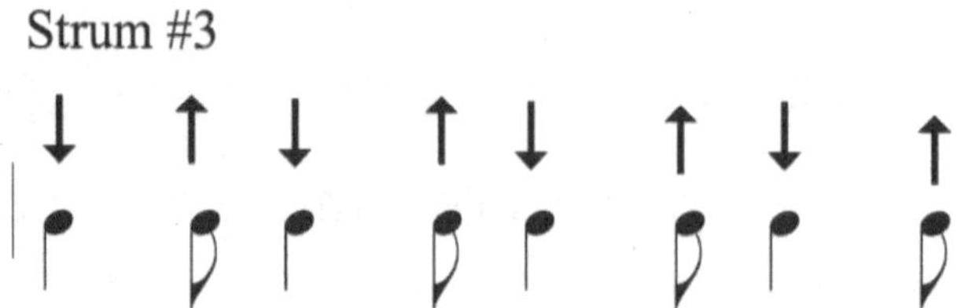

Use the fingernails of your right hand for the down strum and the thumbnail of your right hand for the up strum. Some people also use the pads of their fingers. Do downward strums with the middle three fingers of your right hand. Adjust the angle of your strumming hand so that your fingernails rest gently on String 4, the string closest to the ceiling. Now turn your forearm as if you were rattling a doorknob and allow your fingernails to gently brush down all four strings toward the floor. You may have to experiment to refine your hand shape and the amount of pressure on the strings. Listen to be sure that you are strumming all four strings.

Just in case you were wondering, most uke players do not use a pick because it can break the ukulele's strings. There are felt picks available which will not harm your ukulele's strings.

You should strum across the bottom of the fretboard on the main body of the instrument, NOT where the strings cross over the sound hole in the middle of the instrument. The drawing on the next page shows where your right hand should strum.

Learning these patterns takes time. If your fingers get sore, don't worry. It can take a while to build up thicker skin. We'll suggest some more complicated strumming patterns later in the book that are derived from these three basic patterns.

How to Read Tablature

Lines of the Tab Staff

Each line of the tab staff represents a string on the ukulele. The sounds that are higher in ***pitch*** are closer to the top of the page just as they are on the standard music ***staff***. However, the unfortunate result is that standard tab notation places the lines upside down from how they are arranged on the ukulele.

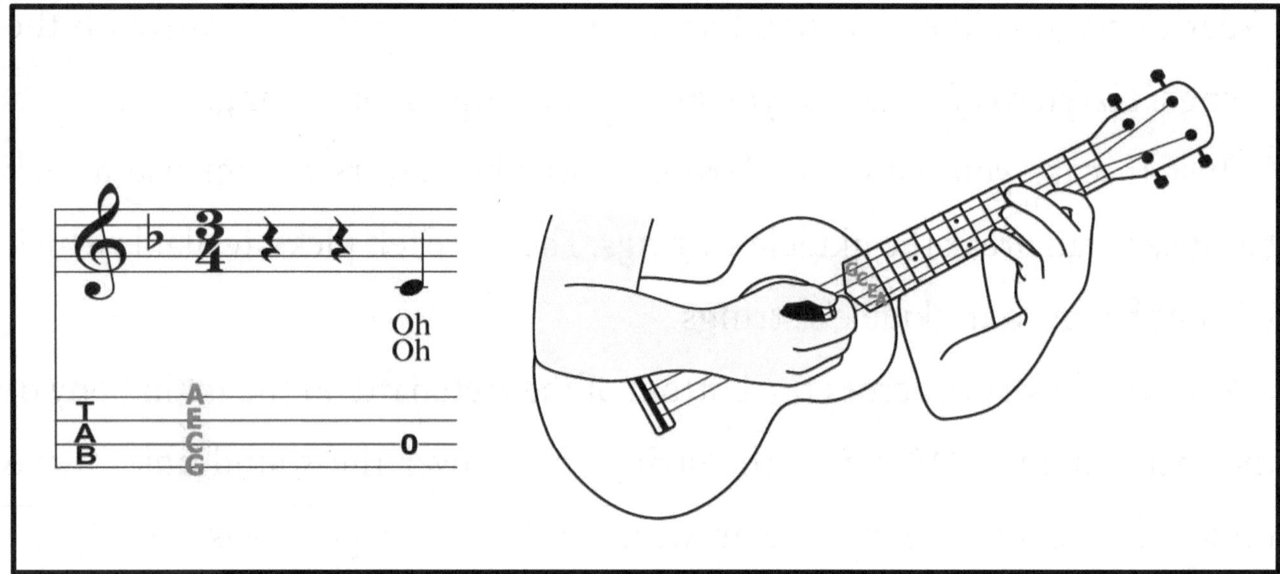

So:

- The top line of the tab staff is the A string (the string closest to the floor when you're playing).
- The line below that is the E string.
- The line below that is the C string.
- The bottom line of the tab is the G string, which is the string closest to the ceiling when you are playing.

Numbers on the Tab Staff

The numbers on the lines of the tab staff tell you which fret to ***stop*** with a left hand finger. ***Stopping*** (also called ***fretting***) a string means to use a left hand finger and push down firmly so that the string contacts the fret. Your finger goes between the frets, not on a fret.

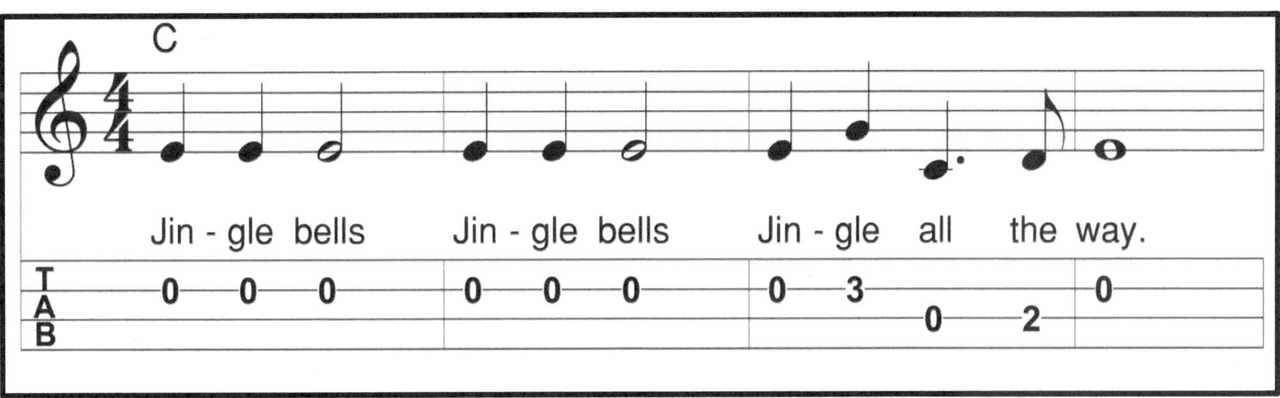

For example, a 5 means to means to put one of your left hand fingers in the fifth fret, and push down on the string as you pluck it with your right hand. A 7 means to stop the string in the 7th fret and pluck it with your right hand. A 4 means to stop the string in the fourth fret and pluck it with your right hand. A 0 means to pluck a string with your right hand without using your left hand at all. We call an unstopped string an ***open string***.

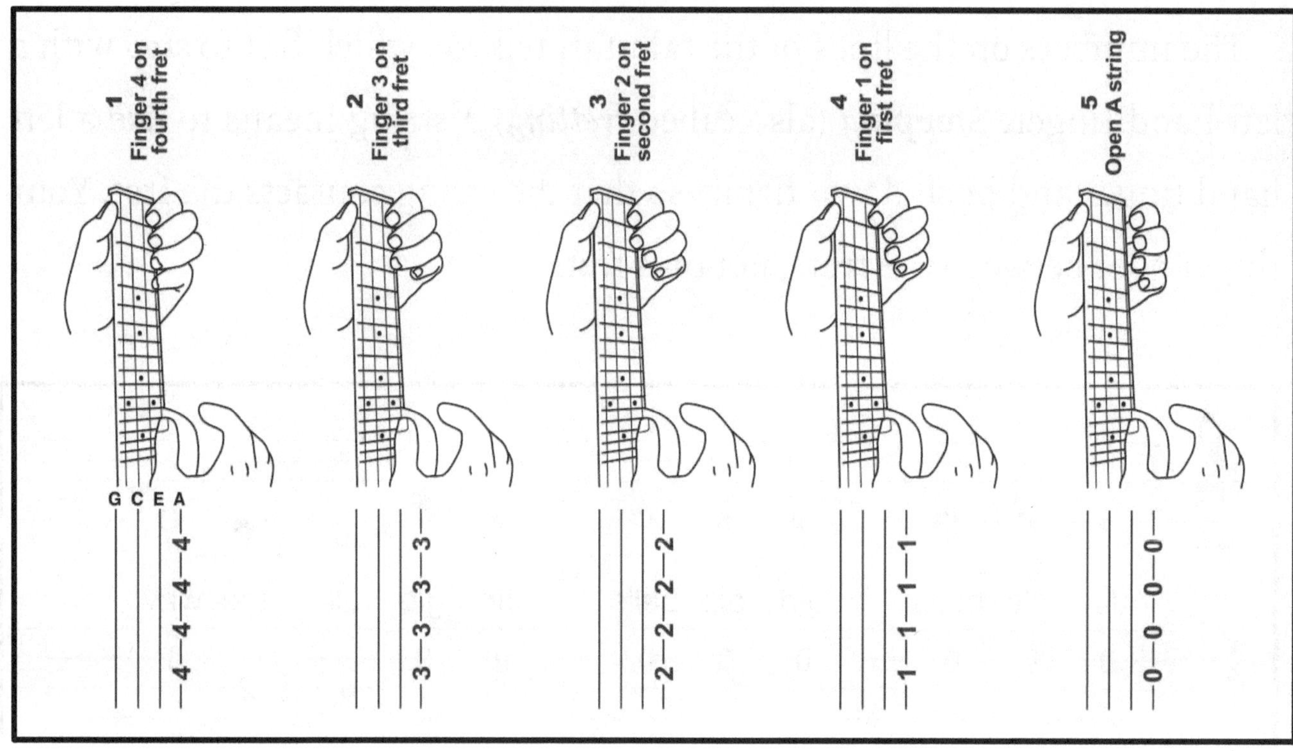

The image above shows a person fretting the A string. Usually, we use finger 1 on the first fret, finger 2 on the second fret, finger 3 on the third fret, and finger 4 on the fourth fret. Having your fingers in this arrangement is referred to as ***first position***.

For practice reading tab, try playing the sounds shown in the parts of the image. Reading from right to left:

1. Start with finger 4 in the fourth fret and pluck the A string 4 times.
2. Then use finger 3 in the third fret and pluck the A string 4 times.
3. Next use finger 2 in the second fret and pluck the A string 4 times
4. Next use finger 1 in the first fret and pluck the A string 4 times.
5. Finally, pluck the open A string 4 times.

Occasionally, you will see numbers above the tab staff in your book. Here is an example.

These numbers are there to help you know which finger of your left hand to use. When you shift your hand up the neck of the ukulele, it is helpful to have as few movements as possible. These fingerings are a suggestion so you don't slide around for every note higher than fret #3.

Playing the C Major Scale in Tab Notation

We recommend practicing the C major scale while reading the tab notation as the next step to getting comfortable with reading and playing tab notation. It will help your brain link the look of the tab staff to the muscular patterns needed to play certain notes. Since most melodies are made from fragments of scales, learning this eye-hand coordination will make it a lot easier for you to read tab melodies.

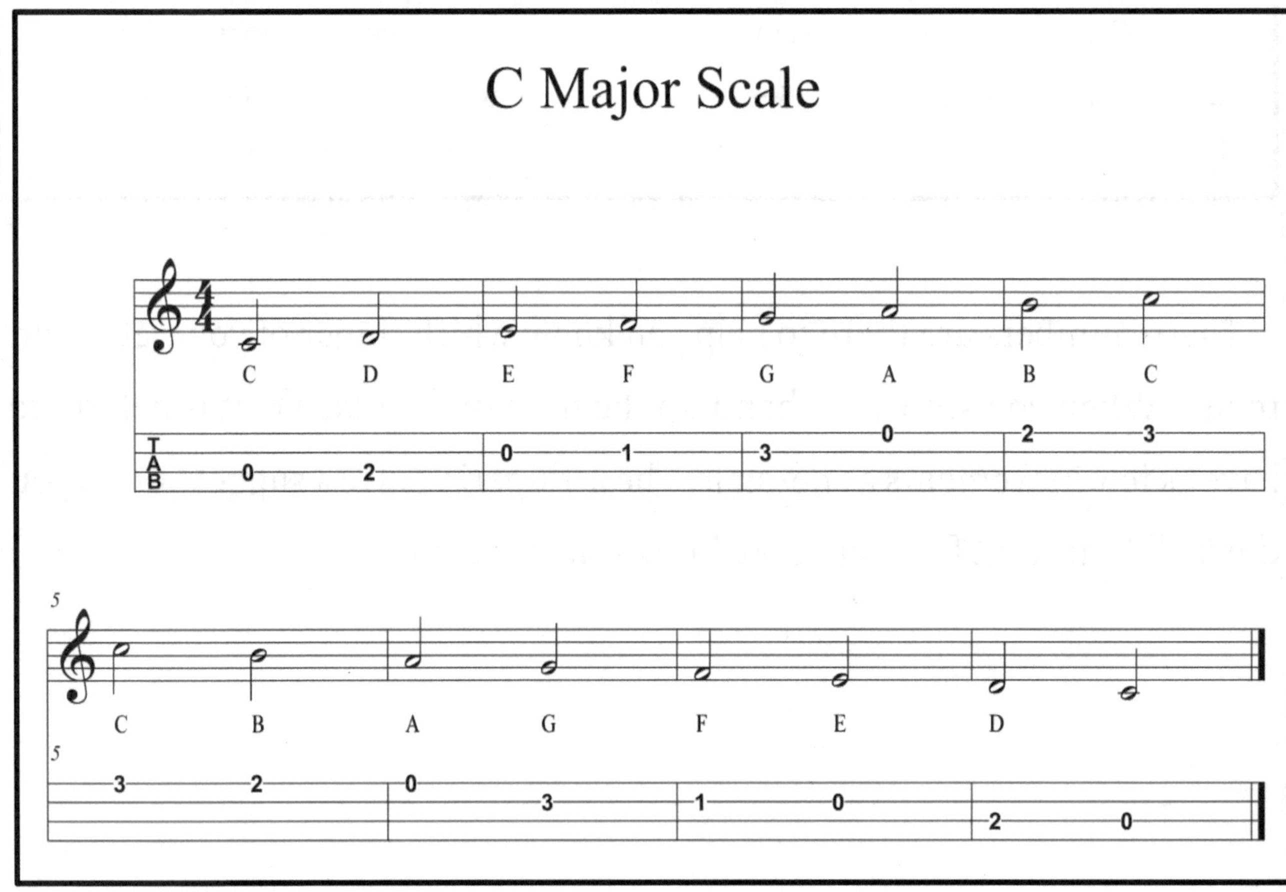

Putting It Together: Reading a Melody in Tab

Our first song is "Oh Christmas Tree." The full song is in the "Two-Chord Christmas Songs" chapter; we've reproduced a part here.

To read the tab, look below the regular staff for the tab staff and see which string line the number is on. Then use your left hand to stop that string in the fret that matches the number shown. Remember that 0 means an open string.

- For the first ***note***, don't do anything with your left hand and pluck the C string with your right hand.
- For the second, third and fourth notes, stop the E string in the first fret.
- For the fifth note, stop the E string in the third fret.

Special Lesson Video Format for Tab Melodies

Your free video course has 21 lesson videos, one for each song in the book. Most have a special onscreen format to help you learn tab. As you watch the video lesson, you'll hear the way the music should sound. You'll also see lots of visual cues to help you link how the tab looks with how the music sounds.

Arrow #1 in the screenshot below points to the tab symbol that corresponds to the note you are hearing. In this example it is a 1, circled in red in the video lesson. You'll see Jenny fretting and plucking the string in the main frame of the video. Arrow #2 points at Jenny's finger fretting the string in the first fret.

Arrow #3 points at a dot on the fretboard at the right of the screen. The dot is supposed to represent your finger. It's also supposed to help you see which string and fret go with the tab symbol.

If you think the ukuleles in the lesson videos sound different from yours, it's not your imagination! We are playing tenor ukuleles in the videos, so our G strings are one octave lower than the soprano ukulele that most folks play. Tab staff doesn't show tenor uke's low G because there's no room for it, but as you train your musical ear you'll be able to hear the difference.

How to Tune Your Ukulele

The main thing to know about tuning your ukulele is that you need to compare the sound of the string you are tuning to a source that you know is in tune. For a pitch source you can use a piano, an online tuner, a tuning app, or a clip-on electric tuner.

Your free video course at ukulele.io has a lesson on how to tune your ukulele inside the "Two-Chord Christmas Songs" unit. Visit the section of this book called "How to Access Your Free Video Course at ukulele.io" for instructions on how to get to your free course.

Adjust your string to match the sound of the source by turning the tuning peg. Don't worry if you're not sure which way to turn the peg – there are only two directions possible, so experiment until your string sounds like the source.

Which direction to turn the peg depends on how the string was attached to the tuning peg by the person who put the string on your uke, so you have to use your ears to figure it out. One thing remains constant; when the string gets tighter, the pitch (sound) goes up, or higher. When the string gets looser, the pitch goes down.

Be sure to pluck the string as you turn the peg! This will help you hear if the sound is getting higher or lower. Also plucking as you turn will help you avoid tightening the string so much that it breaks.

Once you get your string to match the sound of the tuner, try tuning the string's pitch higher and then lower, just to get more practice listening and turning the tuning peg at the same time.

By the way, it's best to first tune your string's pitch slightly lower than the target pitch and then gradually adjust it back up until it matches. As you lower the string's pitch, you're loosening the tension on the string. Then pluck as you turn the peg to adjust the pitch from slightly too low to perfectly in tune.

Tuning this way will help the tension above the tuning peg nut to equal the tension on the instrument's neck. This will help keep the string in tune longer – always a good thing! Don't worry if you didn't understand this last paragraph; as you get more experience tuning your ukulele, you'll understand better how it works.

Fingerpicking Technique

Jenny uses two different ways of fingerpicking the melodies of the songs.

- **Plucking with your index finger:** use this method for a faster moving song. Put your right thumb against the edge of the ***fretboard*** and pluck with your right index finger, pulling the string toward the ceiling to make the sound. This method will give you more rhythmic control and let you play faster.

- **Plucking with your thumb:** use this method for a slower moving song. This method will give you a richer sound.

As you work your way through the book, we'll teach you how to fingerpick chords one note at a time (called "broken" chords). We'll also teach you two techniques for quick moving melody notes. One is called a "hammer on" and the other is called a "pull-off."

One Last Thing: Be Sure to Sign Up for Your Free Video Course!

With purchase of this book you get access to a video course hosted at ukulele.io as a free goodie. Watching the video lessons can make learning the ukulele easier and more fun, so we hope you'll sign up. As the old saying goes, a picture is worth a thousand words, and a video is probably worth a lot more.

In the back of the book is a section with step by step instructions and screenshots to show you how to access your free course at our website, ukulele.io. Or you can visit ukulele.io/access-free-video-course. We're so convinced of the learning value of the video course that we will be happy to set up your account for you. Just shoot us an email at ukulele.io/contact-us/.

If you're thinking, "Why should I be bothered to sign up for the course when I already have the book?" check out what some other customers have to say:

> "You can watch and play along with the video and sound tracks. All the learning procedures are set out to keep you happy, as you watch, listen and learn to play. It's an excellent tutorial programme."
>
> "The videos are charmingly amateurish in a way that makes me think "I can do it too"."
>
> "Between this book and the associated video tutorials, I learned so much so quickly. I was able to pick out some songs (on my ukulele) the first day I messed around with it."

Two-Chord Christmas Songs

"Let's start at the very beginning, a very good place to start."

–Rodgers and Hammerstein

Two-chord songs are definitely a good place to begin with Christmas songs, and here are two of them to get you off to a good start. Each song will be presented as a sing and strum version with the melody and chords written in standard music notation on a treble staff. Underneath the standard musical notation is a line of tab so that you can learn to play the melody of the song too.

Learning F and C7 Chords

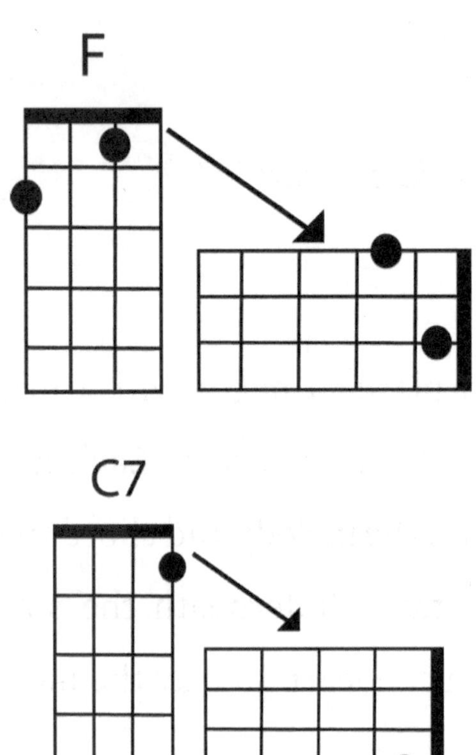

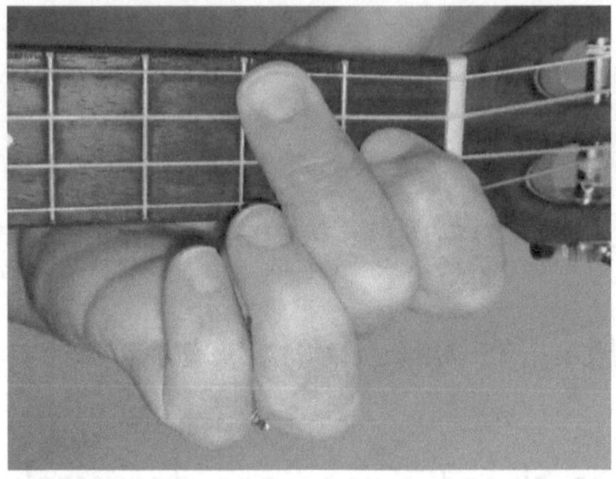

Oh Christmas Tree

This cheerful carol originated in Germany as the folk song, "O Tannenbaum," which is German for fir tree. Although the melody dates back to the sixteenth century, the lyrics weren't written until the early 1800s. German composer Ernst Anschütz wrote the first version of the song in 1819 as a lament about a faithless lover, unflatteringly comparing her with the constant green of the fir tree. In 1824 he converted the song to a Christmas carol, around the time that Christmas trees were becoming a popular custom in Germany. The song eventually found its way to the United States, where its melody became a state song, “Maryland, My Maryland,” in 1861. Although only the English translation of “O Tannenbaum” specifically mentions Christmas, the song is sung during the holiday season on both sides of the Atlantic.

We recommend you use Strum #1 (all down strums) for “Oh Christmas Tree.” For fingerpicking the melody, put your right thumb against the edge of the ***fretboard*** and pluck with your right index finger, pulling the string toward the ceiling to make the sound. This method will help you play faster.

Here’s a quick review of how to read tablature. Each line represents a string on the ukulele. Standard tab notation requires the lines to be placed upside down from how they are arranged on the ukulele. So, the top line of the tab staff is the A string (the string closest to the floor when you're playing), the line below that is the E string, the next line down is C string, and the bottom line of the tab is the G string, which is the string closest to the ceiling when you are playing.

The numbers on the lines tell you which fret to play. A 0 means to pluck a string with your right hand without using your left hand at all. A 1 means to put one of your left-hand fingers in the first fret and push down on the string. So, for the first note, don’t do anything with your left hand and pluck the C string with your right hand. For the second, third and fourth notes, stop the E string in the first fret. For the fifth note, stop the E string in the third fret. Be sure to watch the video in your free course to see how the tab symbols translate into movement and sound.

Oh Christmas Tree
Strumming Pattern:
↓ ↓ ↓
F
C7
F
Oh Christ-mas tree, Oh Christ - mas tree, thy
Oh Christ-mas tree, Oh Christ - mas tree, such
C7
F
F
leaves are so un - chang-ing, Oh Christ-mas tree, Oh
plea - sure do you bring me, Oh Christ-mas tree, Oh
C7
F
Christ - mas tree, thy leaves are so un - chang-ing. Not
Christ - mas tree, such plea - sure do you bring me! For

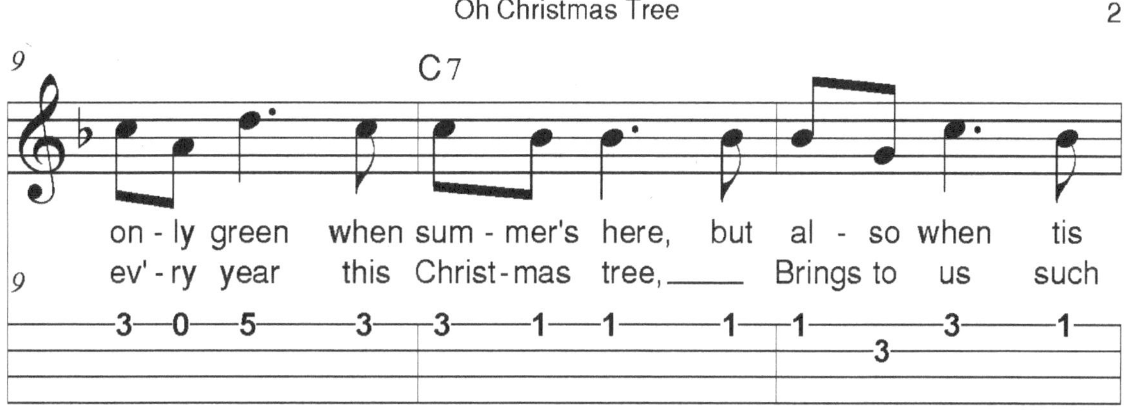
Oh Christmas Tree
2
9
C7
on - ly green when sum - mer's here, but al - so when tis
ev' - ry year this Christ-mas tree, Brings to us such

12
F
cold and drear, Oh Christ-mas tree, Oh Christ-mas tree, thy
joy and glee, Oh Christ-mas tree, Oh Christ-mas tree, such

15
C7
F
leaves are so un - chang - ing.
plea - sure do you bring me.

I Saw Three Ships

This folk carol originated in England, probably in the fifteenth century. Very little is known about its origin. It may be based on an obscure German legend from 1162, when three ships are said to have sailed into Cologne bearing relics from the journey of the Three Wise Men at the time of the birth of Christ. The song itself doesn't mention the Wise Men, though – the three ships refer to the Holy Family of Jesus, Mary, and Joseph. Although a song about ships seems a bit odd for an event that occurred in Bethlehem in the Middle East, the melody is likable and easy to play on the ukulele.

For this song, you can choose from three different strumming patterns.

Strum 1 (all down strums) is the easiest.

Strum 3 (uneven down-up) works with the rhythm of the song since it is in 6/8 time.

Fancy Triplet Strum In the video lesson, Jenny shows how to do a triplet strum. This pattern is a down strum with the index finger, followed by a down stroke with the thumb and then an up stroke with the thumb. It makes a cool effect, but you need to practice it! Strumming up and down with your fingers rather than the whole arm will allow you to create a group of three strums at a faster speed.

I Saw Three Ships

Strumming Pattern
↓ ↑↓ ↑↓ ↑↓ ↑

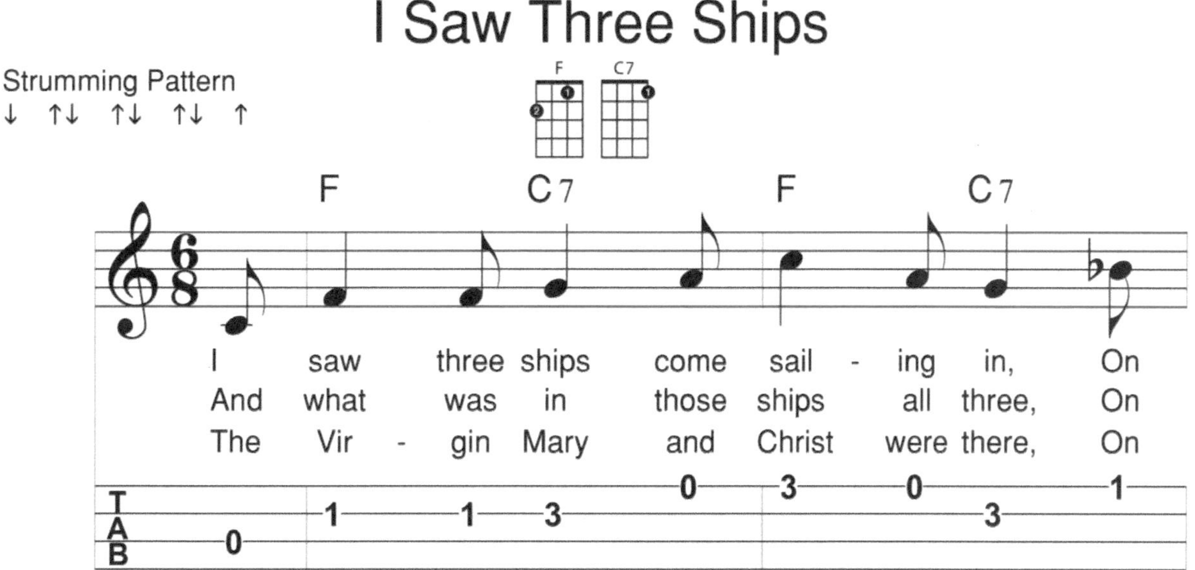

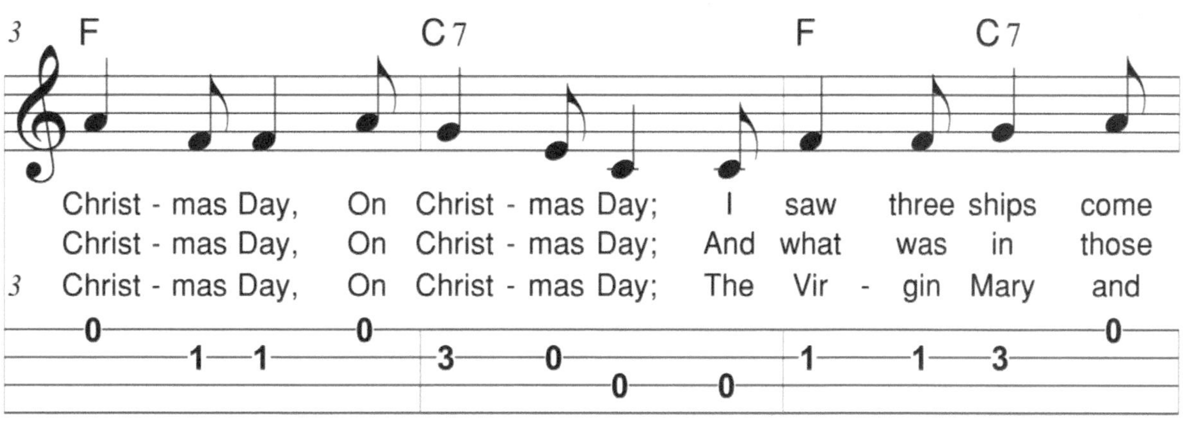

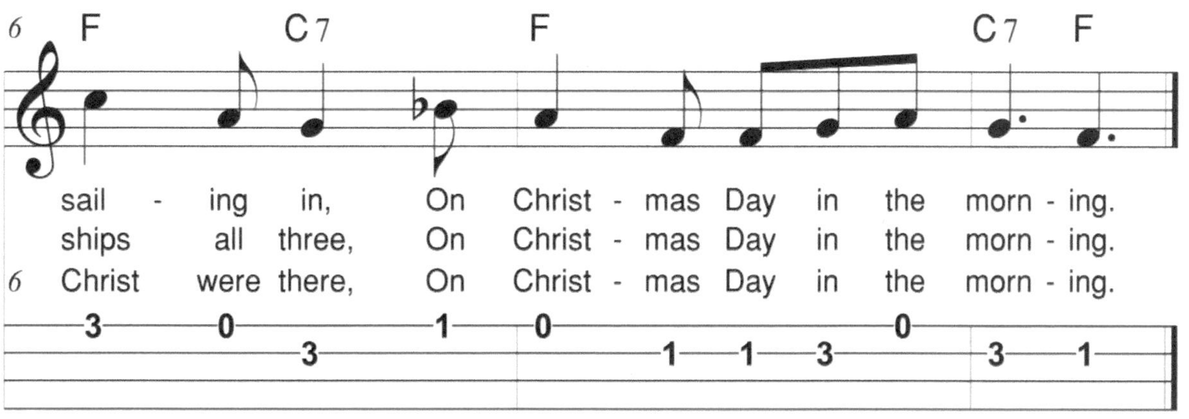

I Saw Three Ships

Three-Chord Christmas Songs

The three chords used in the songs in this chapter are C, F and G7. You've learned how to play the F chord in the previous chapter so here are the C and G7 chords:

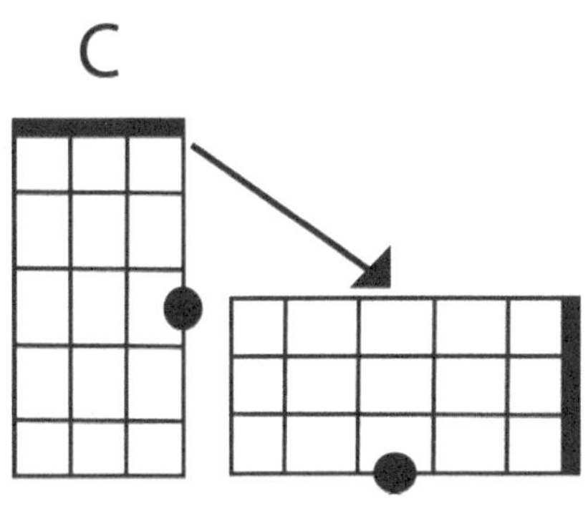

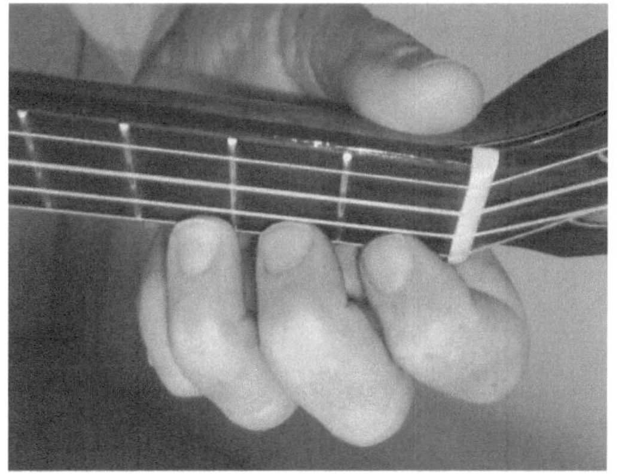

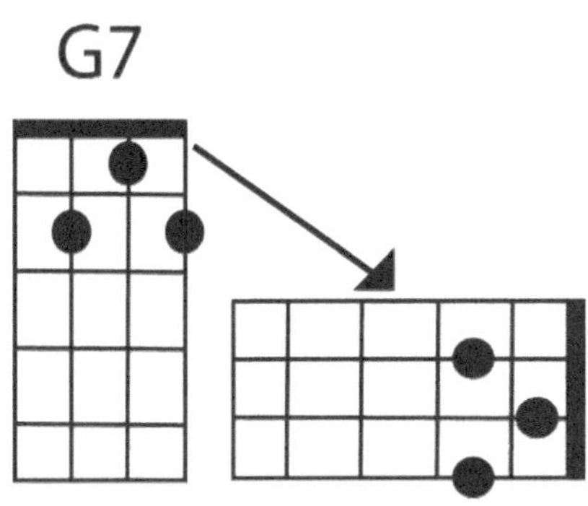

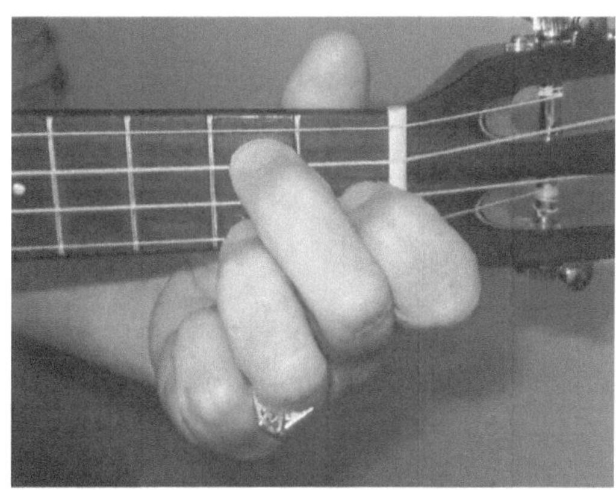

If you've never played ukulele before, you may find the G7 chord challenging. Another skill that new players struggle with is being able to change the chords quickly and at the right time in the song. There is a video in your free course at ukulele.io called "How to Play the G7 Chord" that can help you learn this chord. The video also shows how to change chords from C to G7.

If you find playing these Christmas songs very challenging, you might want to work through our first book, *21 Songs in 6 Days: Learn Ukulele the Easy Way*. We'll walk you through learning five basic chords and give you lots of practice on changing chords quickly and keeping your strumming going. Here's an easy link to pick up a copy: ukulele.io/Buy21songs.

Jingle Bells

Written in Boston in 1857, this song is not only an American Christmas carol, but a distinctly New England one. Listening to the melody, you can almost hear the clop-clop of the horses' hooves and the ringing of sleigh bells. The composer, James S. Pierpont, wrote "Jingle Bells" for a Sunday school program, but the song's theme is secular, and in fact it's probably the first secular Christmas song composed in the United States. Because sheet music versions often reference J. Pierpont as the author, the eighteenth-century Connecticut composer John Pierpont sometimes mistakenly gets credit for writing it. Even though it doesn't contain a single reference to Christmas, "Jingle Bells" is probably the world's most popular Christmas song.

Since you probably know the melody very well, this is a great song to try learning to fingerpick the melody. Playing the chorus ("Jingle Bells, Jingle Bells, jingle all the way") is pretty easy because it stays in the ***first position***. Playing the verse ("Dashing through the snow") is a lot harder because of the necessary position shifts with your left hand. Use the dots on the side of your ukulele's fretboard to help you gauge the distances. You can also only fingerpick the chorus and strum and sing the verses.

If you haven't watched any lesson videos yet, "Jingle Bells" is a good one to start with because Claire the Cat insistently participates in the lesson. We recommend using Strum #1 for this song, which is all down strums.

Jingle Bells

Strumming Pattern:
↓ ↓ ↓ ↓

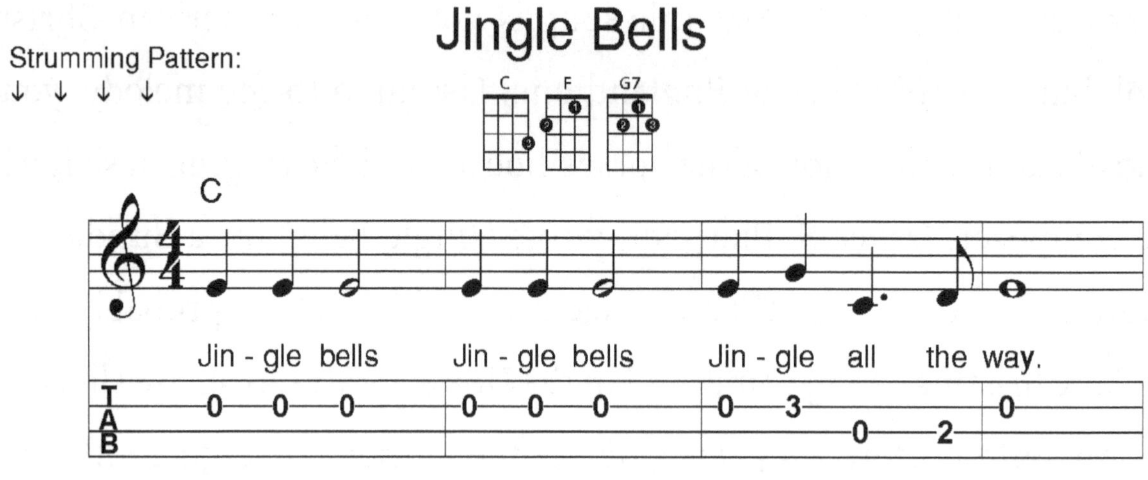

F
Dash - ing through the snow, In a one horse o - pen sleigh.
day or two a - go, I thought I'd take a ride. And
G7
C
O'er the fields we go, Laughing all the way.
soon Miss Fan - ny Bright was seat - ed at my side. The
F
Bells on bob - tail ring. Mak - ing spi - rits bright, What
horse was lean and lank. Mis - for - tune seemed his lot, We
D.C. al Fine
G7
C
fun it is to ride and sing a sleigh-ing song to - night - Oh!
got in - to a drift - ed bank and then we go up sot - Oh!

This page is intentionally left blank to avoid unnecessary page turns.

O Come, Little Children

The original German title of this song is "Ihr Kinderlein, Kommet." The lyrics were written by German Catholic priest Christoph von Schmid in 1801. Johann Abraham Peter Schulz, a German-born composer of some note, set von Schmid's words to music using a tune he composed while serving in the court of the King of Denmark a few years earlier. This carol celebrates the birth of Jesus by beckoning all children (and the child within each of us) to stand beside the innocent babe in the manger. It's a lovely metaphor and easy to add to your Christmas repertoire.

Use Strum #1 to quickly learn the lyrics and chords for this simple song. Once you've got the hang of the lyrics and chords, try this new strumming pattern: down, down-up-down, down-up. Each down strum comes on a beat of the music – all the down strums should be equally spaced in time – with each single up strum halfway between two down strums.

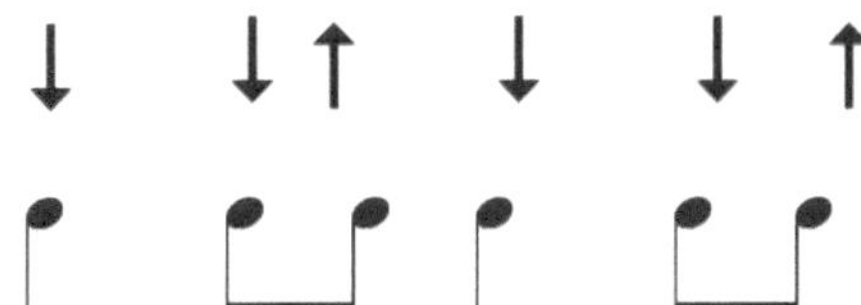

Be sure to watch the video for this song to get a feel for the rhythm. This new pattern is more complicated to learn because the amount of time after a down strum is different than the amount of time after an up strum.

O Come, Little Children

Strumming Pattern:
↓ ↓↑ ↓ ↓↑

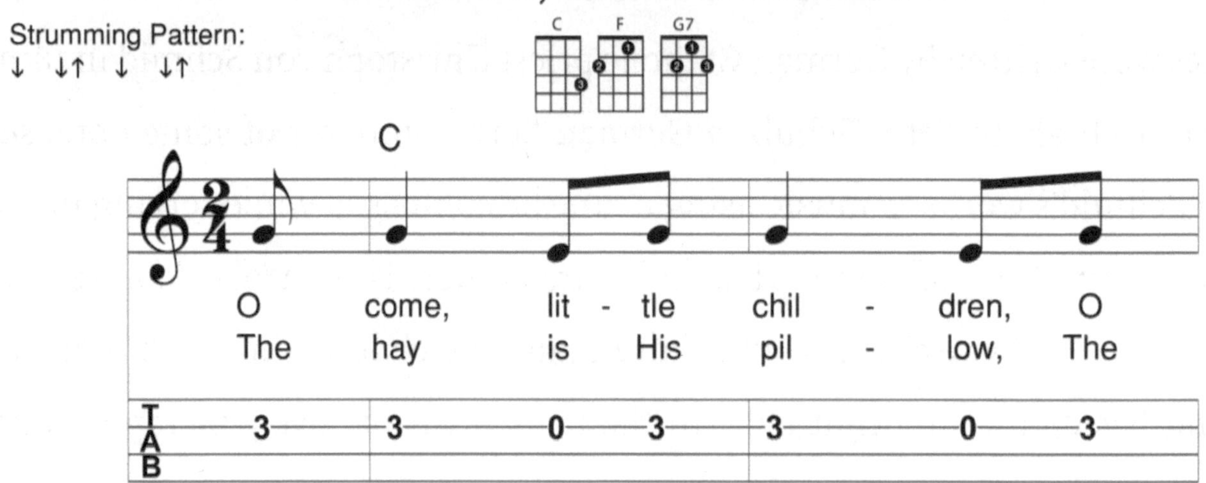

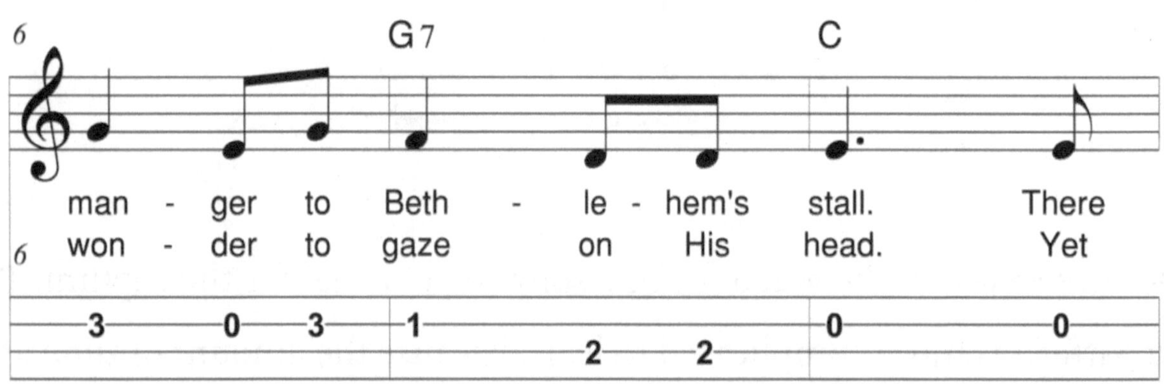

O Come, Little Children 2

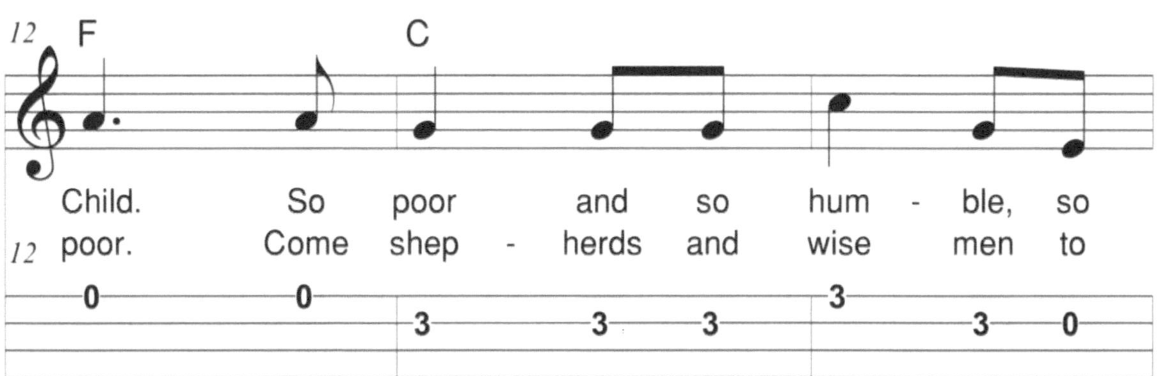

Good King Wenceslas

To appreciate "Good King Wenceslas," you need to accept a bit of artistic license. The beautiful melody dates back to the Middle Ages in Europe and was first written as a song about spring. In the 1800s, John Mason Neale, an English poet, added the lyrics and turned it into a Christmas carol. There really was a nobleman named Wenceslas. However, he was a duke, not a king, and he lived in tenth-century Bohemia rather than England. And while his name was Wenceslas, it would have been pronounced Vaclav in Czech. He did do many good deeds until his brother murdered him in a family struggle for political power. Afterward he was considered a martyr and was declared the patron saint of Bohemia, now the Czech Republic. Although the song doesn't mention the Christmas holiday, its theme of compassion for the poor is an enduring message for every Christmas season. By the way, the Feast of Stephen is celebrated on December 26th to commemorate Saint Stephen, the first Christian martyr.

We've included a second tab version for this song so you can fingerpick the chords, which gives the song a nice medieval flavor to match the era of the tune. To make a great sounding accompaniment, your left hand continues to make the same chord shapes that you make when you are strumming while your right hand plucks one string at a time in a rhythmic pattern. Study the tab so you pluck the strings in the following order: G, A, C, E. An easier way to remember the order is that you pluck the outer strings first (going from bottom to top) and then the inner strings once (also from bottom to top). So, you could chant "out, out, in, in" to keep track of what to do. Or just watch the lesson video in your free course.

Good King Wenceslas

Strumming Pattern:
↓↑↓↑↓↑↓↑

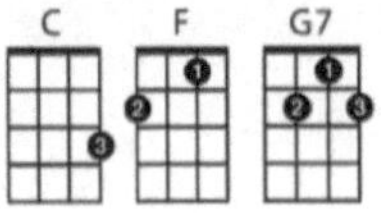

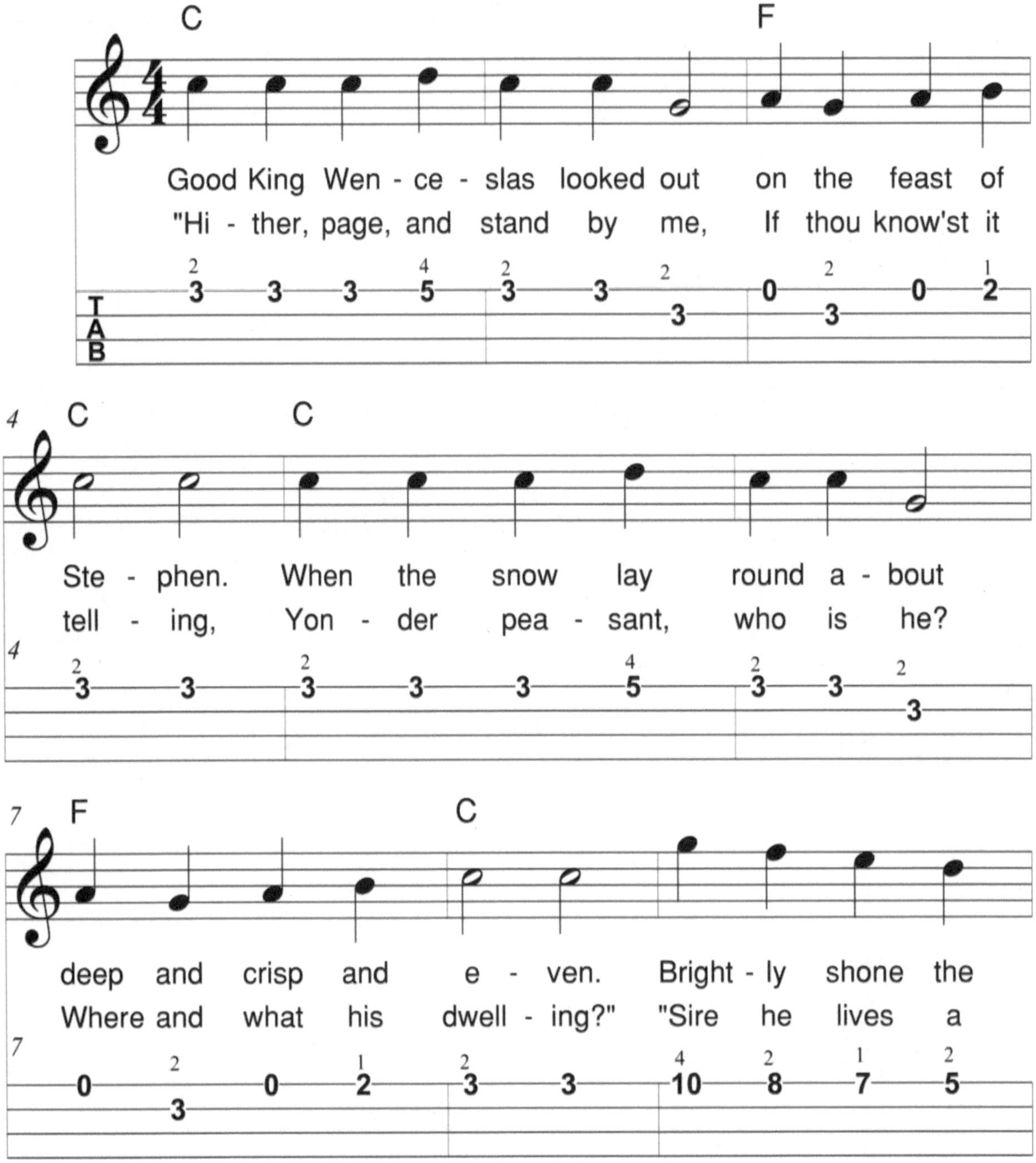

C | F

Good King Wen - ce - slas looked out on the feast of
"Hi - ther, page, and stand by me, If thou know'st it

4 C | C

Ste - phen. When the snow lay round a - bout
tell - ing, Yon - der pea - sant, who is he?

7 F | C

deep and crisp and e - ven. Bright - ly shone the
Where and what his dwell - ing?" "Sire he lives a

Good King Wenceslas 2

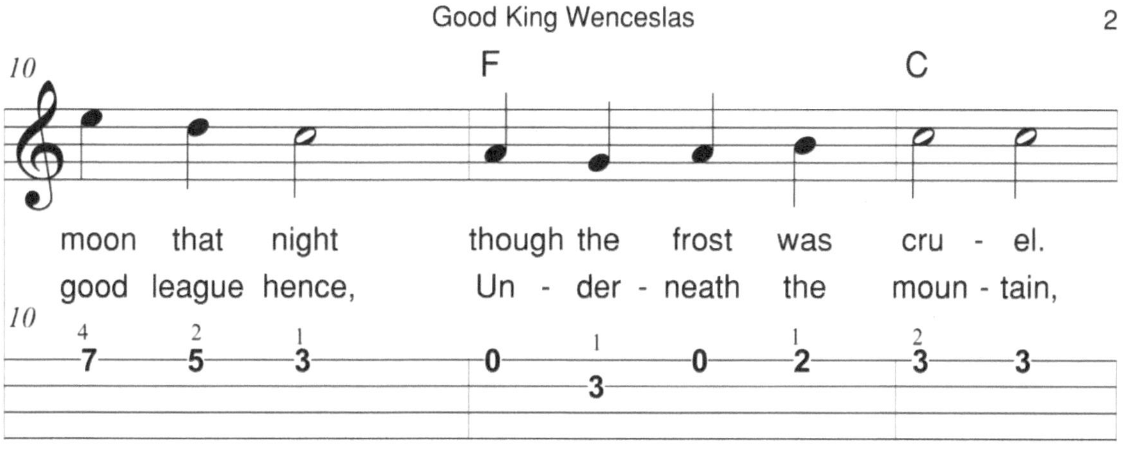

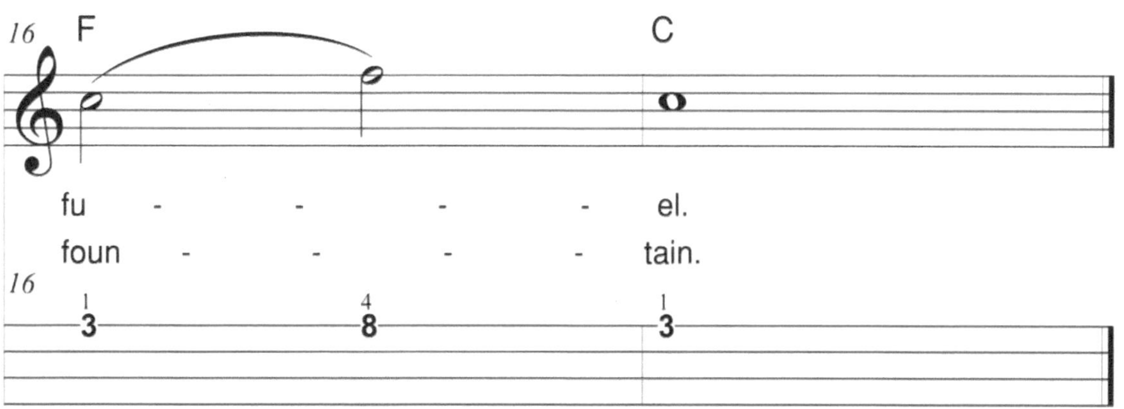

Good King Wenceslas Melody
Finger Picking Accompaniment
Arr. Jenny Peters
C F G7
Good King Wen - ce - slas looked out on the feast of
"Hith - er, page, come stand by me. if thou know'st it
Ste - phen. When the snow lay round a - bout
tell - ing? Yon - der pea - sant, who is he?
deep and crisp and e - ven. Bright - ly shone the
Where and what his dwell - ing. "Sire, he lives a

Good King Wenceslas
2
F C
moon that night though the frost was cru - el.
good league hence, un - der - neath the moun - tain,
F G7 C
When a poor man came in sight, gath - ring win - ter
Right a - gainst the fo - rest fence By Saint Ag - nes
F C
fu - - - el.
foun - - - tain."

This page is intentionally left blank to avoid unnecessary page turns.

Up on the Housetop

It's hard to resist this sprightly little children's carol with its vision of jolly Santa on the roof, ready to descend through the chimney with his enormous bag of Christmas toys. It was written in the 1860s by the Midwestern composer Benjamin R. Hanby. "Up on the Housetop" is second only to "Jingle Bells" as one of the earliest secular American Christmas songs. We can only hope that "good old Santa Claus" has a couple of ukuleles stashed away in his bag of Christmas joys.

When you are first learning this song, use Strum #1. Once you've got the hang of the lyrics and chords, try the strum you first learned in "O Come Little Children."

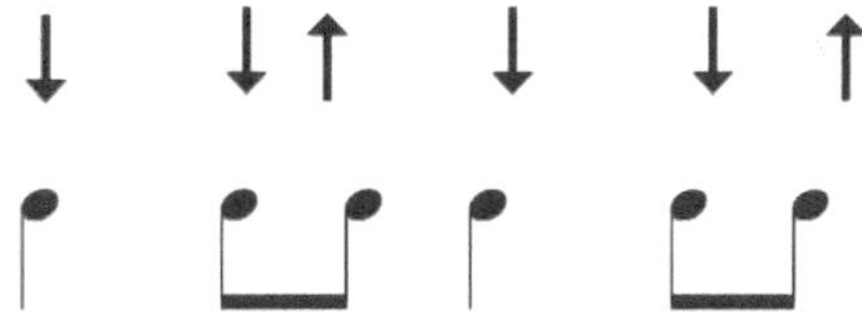

Up On the Housetop
Strumming Pattern:
↓ ↓↑ ↓ ↓↑
C F G7
C F C
Up on the house_ top rein-deer pause, Out jumps good old
First comes the stock-ing of lit - tle Nell, Oh dear San - ta
G7 C
San - ta Claus Down through the chim - ney with lots of toys
fill it well, Give her a doll that_ laughs and cries
F C G7 C F
All for the lit - tle ones Christ-mas joys Ho, ho, ho,
One that will o - pen and shut her eyes Ho, ho, ho,

Up On the Housetop 2

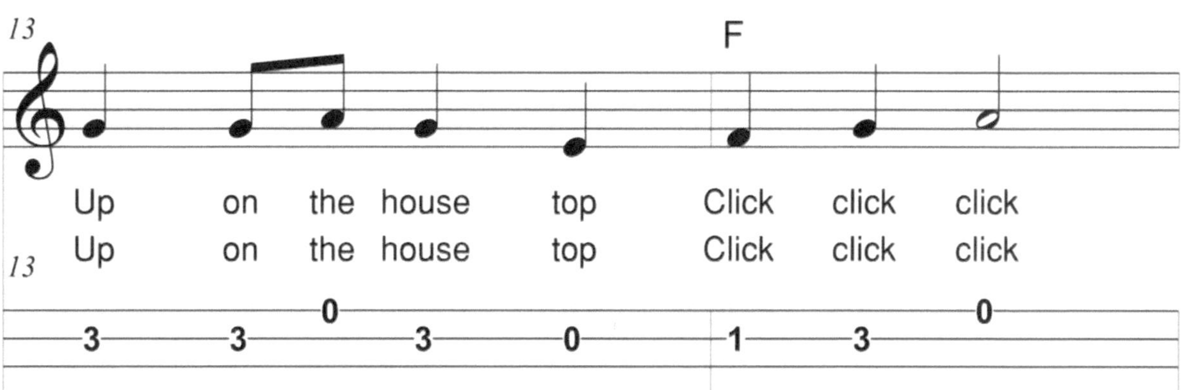

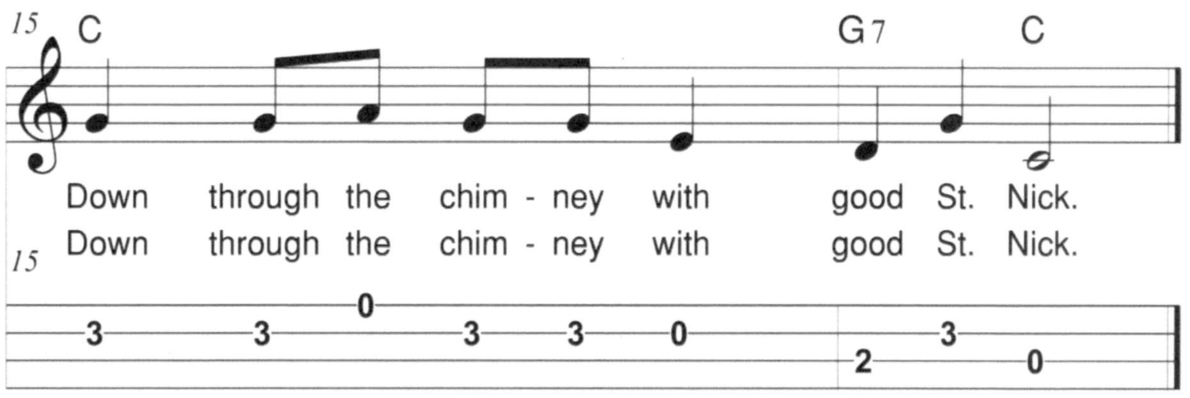

This page is intentionally left blank to avoid unnecessary page turns.

Away in a Manger

The rich imagery of the Nativity in this carol makes it a favorite at Christmas pageants and worship services. Its request for the Lord Jesus to "stay by my cradle 'til morning is nigh" gives it the ring of a child's bedtime prayer or lullaby. The song is often attributed to Martin Luther, with the claim that he wrote it as a hymn for his children. Although Luther did write songs for his children, he didn't write "Away in a Manger." It was written by the American composer James Ramsey Murray in 1887, a few centuries after Luther's time.

"Away in a Manger" is a lullaby, so you should play it at a relaxed tempo. This song is in 3/4 time, also known as waltz time. You could use Strum #1 – all downs – or you could get a little more ambitious and try the new down, down-up, down pattern shown below. Each down strum comes on a beat of the music – all the down strums should be equally spaced in time – with the single up strum halfway between the two down strums, between the second and third beats.

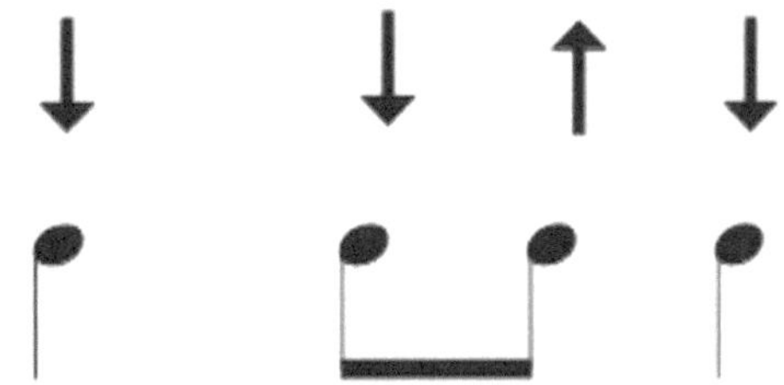

Away in a Manger

Away in a Manger 2

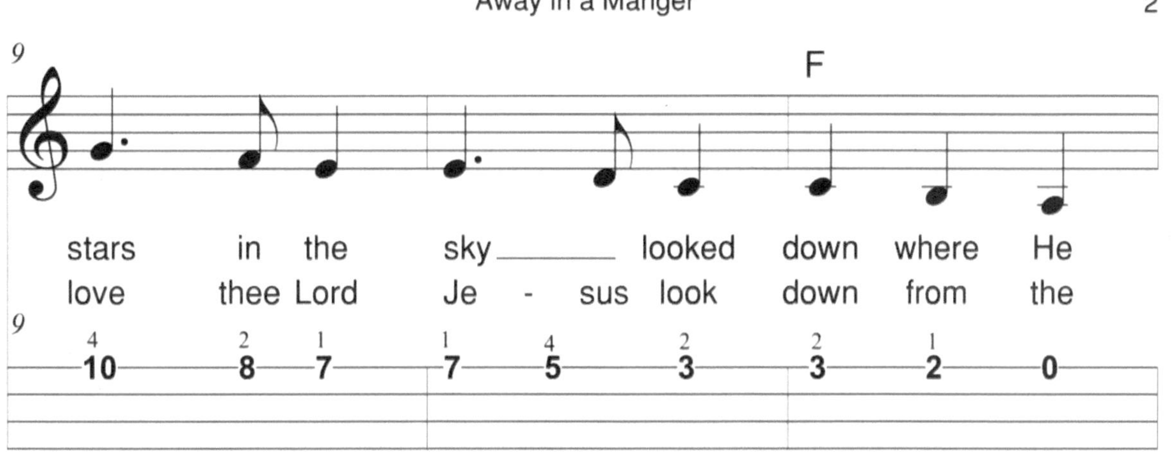

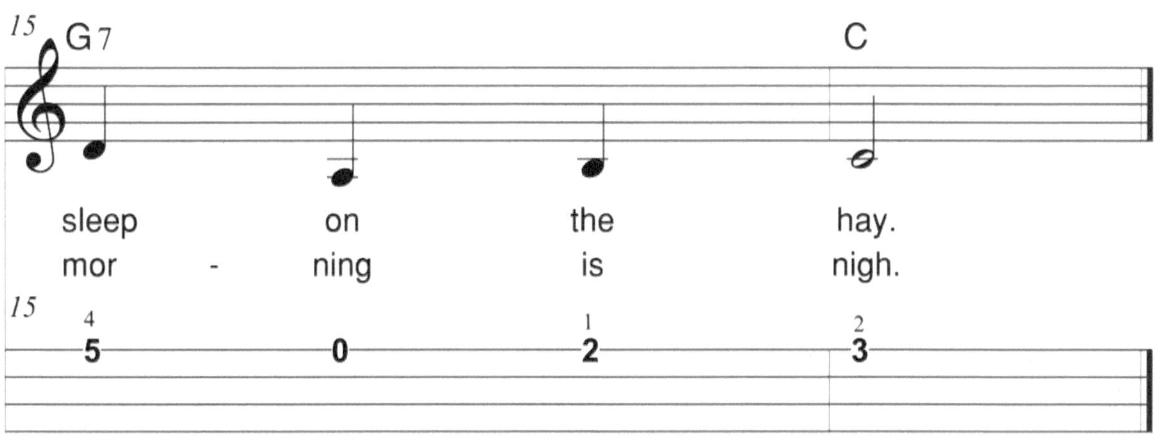

This page is intentionally left blank to avoid unnecessary page turns.

Over the River and Through the Wood

While the chords in this song are the same as the previous two, this song presents a new challenge. Because the rhythm or feel of the song is different, you might find maintaining a steady strum challenging. Try starting with the steady down strums of Strum #1. If you've mastered Strum #1 on this song, try jazzing things up with Strum #3. Finally, if you're ready for a challenge, watch the lesson video to learn how to do a triplet strum.

This song was originally published as a poem in 1844 to celebrate the author's memories of visiting her grandmother at Thanksgiving. Lydia Maria Child was a teacher, writer, and prominent abolitionist in the American pre-Civil War era. Her poem was later set to music by an unknown composer. The song's vivid images of traveling by horse-drawn sleigh predate "Jingle Bells," and could have been the inspiration for it. Depending on which holiday you're celebrating, it's easy to exchange "Thanksgiving" with "Christmas" in the lyrics of "Over the River" without much change in the rhythm.

Over the River and Through the Wood

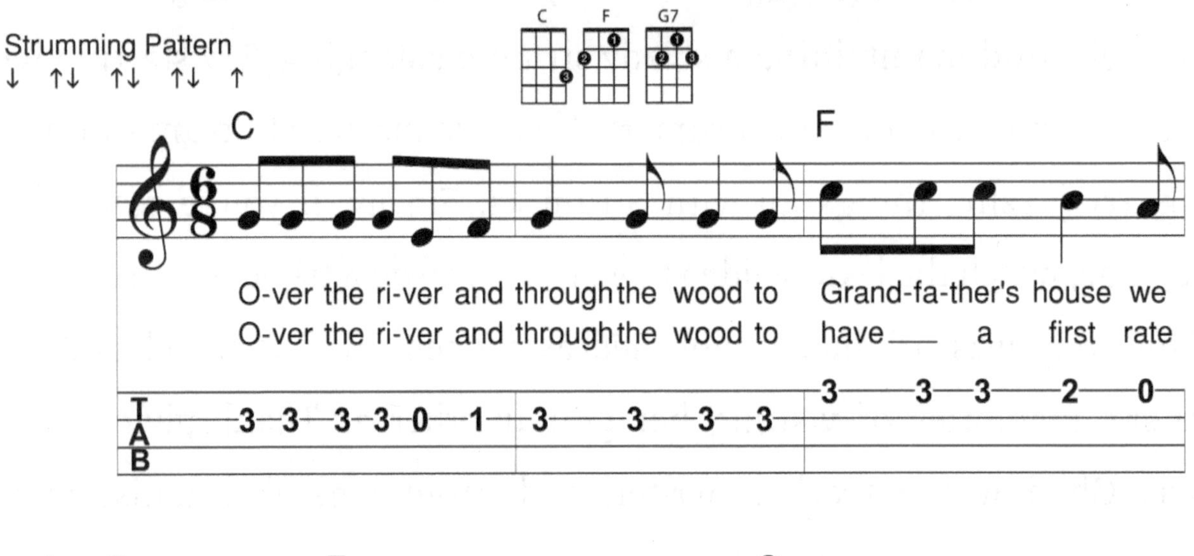

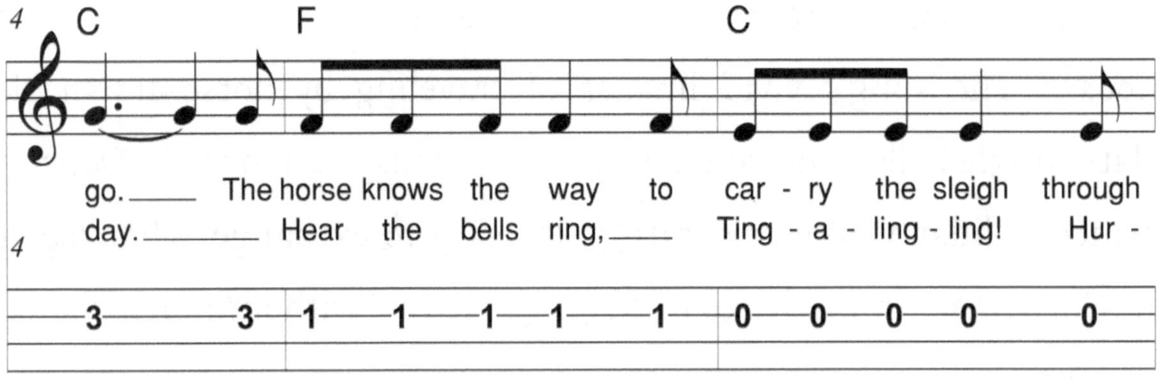

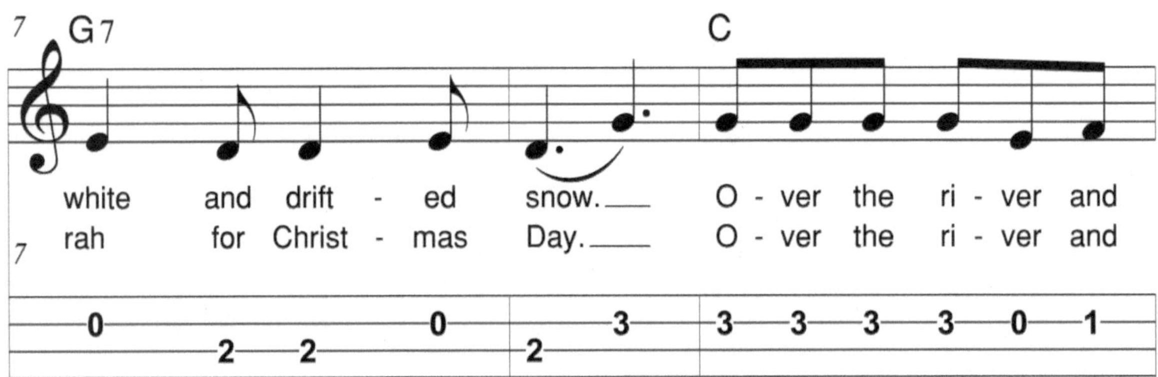

Over the River and Through the Wood 2

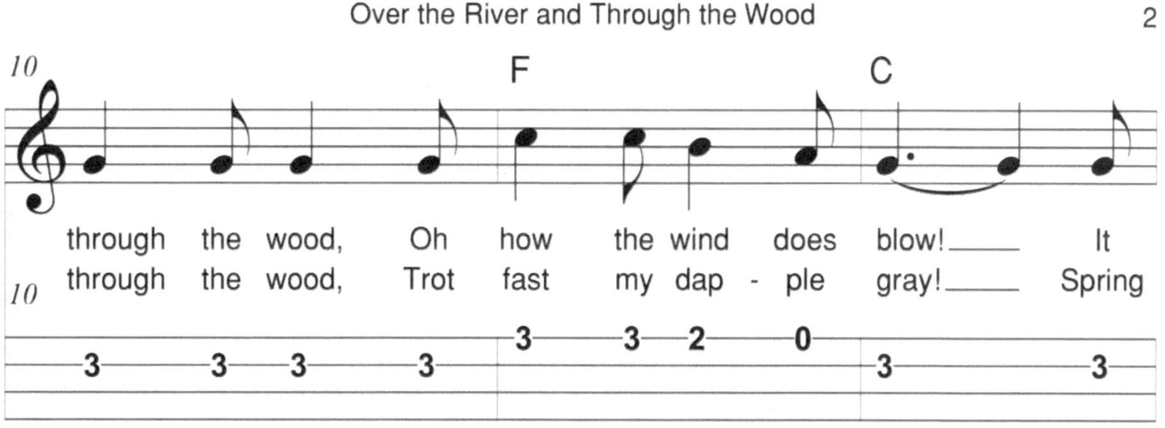

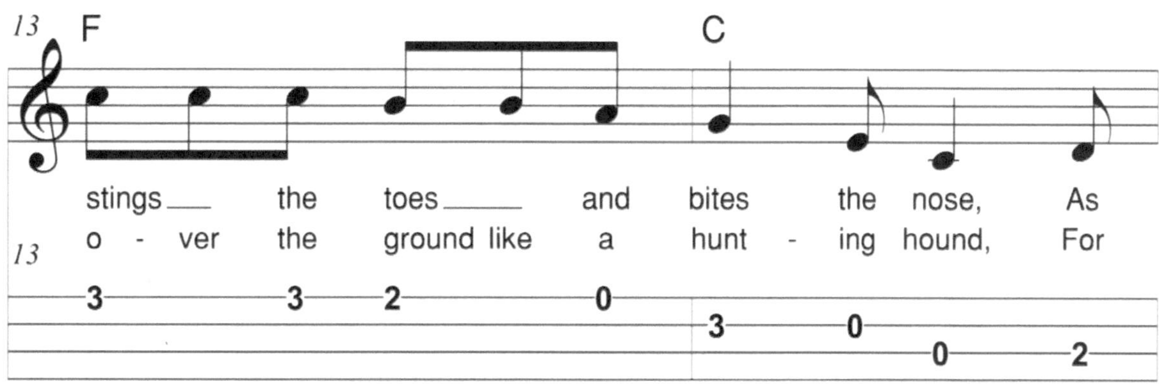

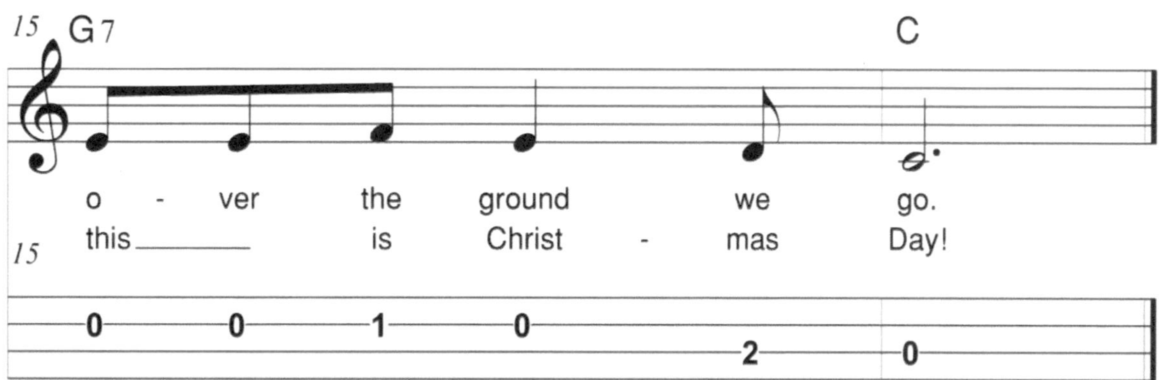

This page is intentionally left blank to avoid unnecessary page turns.

Silent Night

The title of this beloved Christmas carol sounds even more poetic in its original German: "Stille Nacht, Heilige Nacht." It was first performed in 1818 on Christmas Eve in St. Nicholas' Church in Oberndof near Salzburg, Austria. The musical heritage of the Salzburg area includes such legendary figures as Mozart and the Trapp Family Singers who inspired "The Sound of Music," so it's only fitting that "Silent Night" was created there. Father Joseph Mohr, the priest at St. Nicholas', discovered on Christmas Eve that the church organ was unplayable, so he hurriedly wrote the lyrics and rushed them to Franz Xaver Gruber, the church organist in a neighboring village. Gruber set them to music in time for the midnight service.

Since "Silent Night" is 3/4 time, you can use the down, down-up, down strumming pattern we suggested for "Away in a Manger."

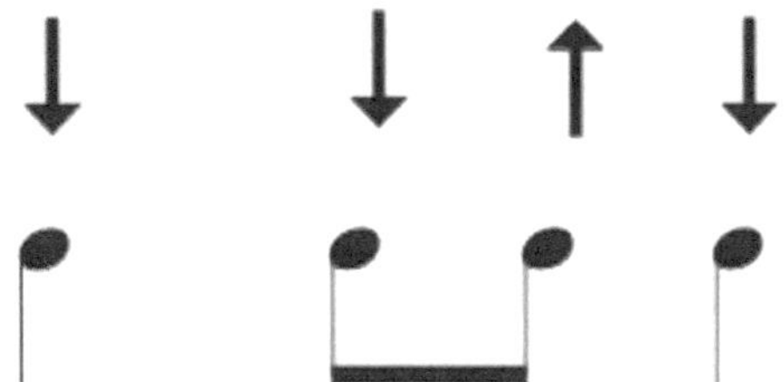

Although the original performance featured a guitar to replace the ailing organ, you can reenact it with your ukulele. Use the tab version to learn how to fingerpick the chords to accompany the melody. You can either sing the melody or have someone play it on their ukulele. A picture is worth a thousand words, so please be sure to watch the lesson video if you are at all confused about how to fingerpick a broken chord.

Silent Night

Strumming Pattern:
↓ ↓↑ ↓

Franz Gruber

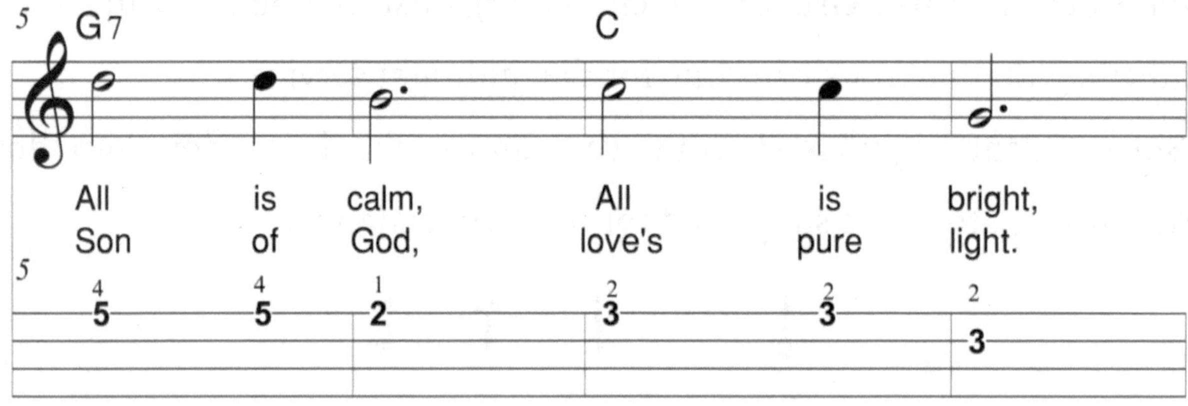

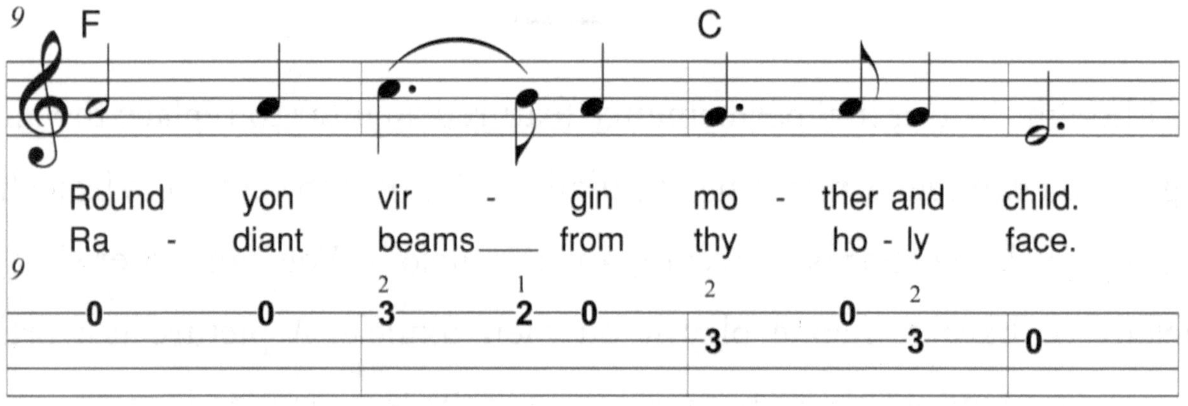

Silent Night
2
13
F
C
Ho - ly in - fant so ten - der and mild.
With the dawn of re - deem - ing grace.
13
0 0 3 2 0 3 0 3 0

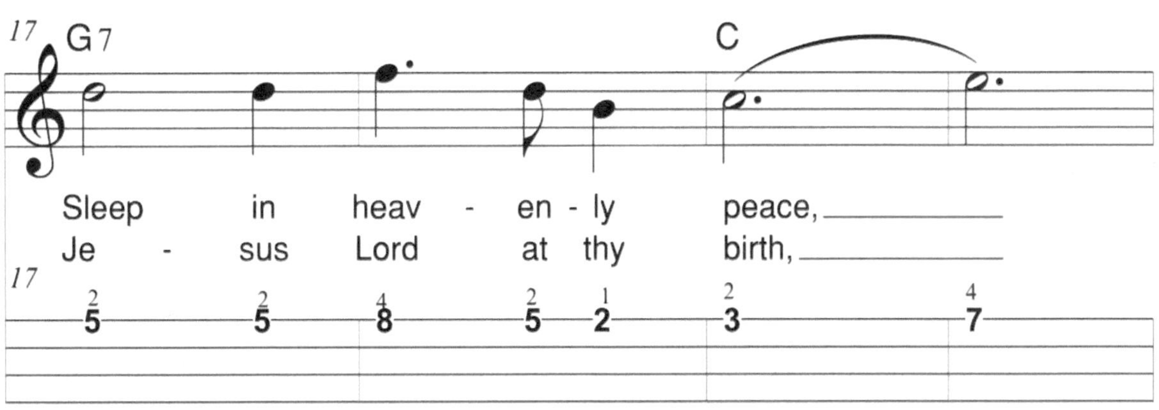
17
G7
C
Sleep in heav - en - ly peace,
Je - sus Lord at thy birth,
17
5 5 8 5 2 3 7

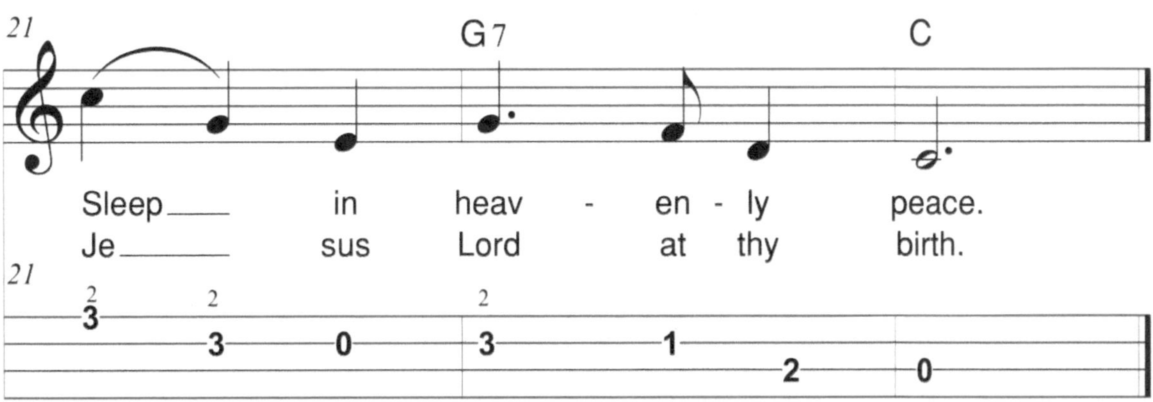
21
G7
C
Sleep in heav - en - ly peace.
Je sus Lord at thy birth.
21
3 3 0 3 1 2 0

C
F
G7
Silent Night
Finger Picking Accompaniment
Franz Gruber
Jenny Peters
Si - lent night, Ho - ly night,
Si - lent night, Ho - ly night,
All is calm, All is bright.
Son of God, love's pure light.
Round yon vir - gin moth - er and child.
Ra - diant beams from thy ho - ly face.

Silent Night
2
13
F
C
Ho - ly in - fant so ten - der and mild.
With the dawn of re - deem - ing grace.
17
G7
C
Sleep in heav - en - ly peace,
Je - sus Lord at thy birth
21
C
G7
C
Sleep - in heav - en - ly peace
Je - sus Lord at thy birth.

This page is intentionally left blank to avoid unnecessary page turns.

Joy to the World

This Christmas hymn triumphantly announces the birth of Christ. It's a work of superb musicianship with classical overtones. The lyrics were adapted from Psalm 98 in 1719 by the English lyricist Isaac Watts, a prolific writer who penned over 700 hymn lyrics as well 60 religious books. The music has been attributed to Handel's "Messiah," but despite the musical similarity, it's far more likely that the tune is American in origin. The American composer Lowell Mason was well trained in classical music and probably set Watts' lyrics to music around 1839. The result is a delight to sing and play.

The ***tempo*** of this song moves fast. When you are fingerpicking the melody, there's a special technique called a "hammer on" to make it easier to play the notes quickly. Watch the video lesson for Jenny's demonstration of how to place a second left hand finger on the fretboard to change the pitch of the string *after* you've plucked it with the right hand.

You can learn how to play easy ukulele chord melody versions of "Jingle Bells," "Up on the Housetop," "Over the River and Through the Wood," "Oh Christmas Tree" and "Silent Night" with our online course *Learn Easy Ukulele Chord Melody Today!* Chord melody is also called 'solo ukulele'. It means that you play both the melody and the chords on your ukulele at the same time. Visit ukulele.io/EasyChordMelody to learn more.

Joy to the World
Strumming Pattern:
↓↑↓↑↓↑↓↑
C F G7
C G7
Joy to the world! The Lord is
Joy to the world! The Sav - ior
He rules the world! With Truth and
C F G7
come; Let earth re - ceive her
reigns; Let men their songs em -
grace, And makes the na - tions
C F C
king; Let ev 'ry heart pre -
ploy. While field and floods, rocks,
prove The glo - ries of His

Joy to the World 2

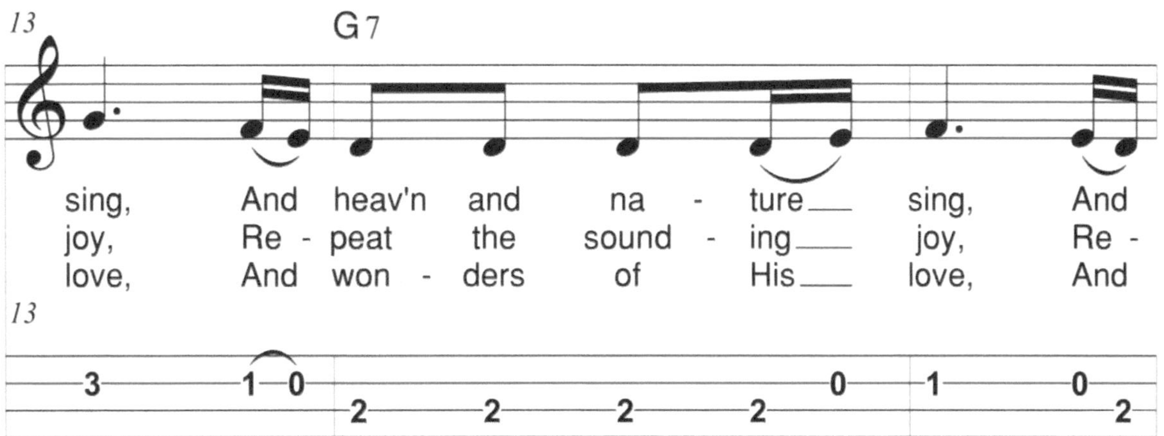

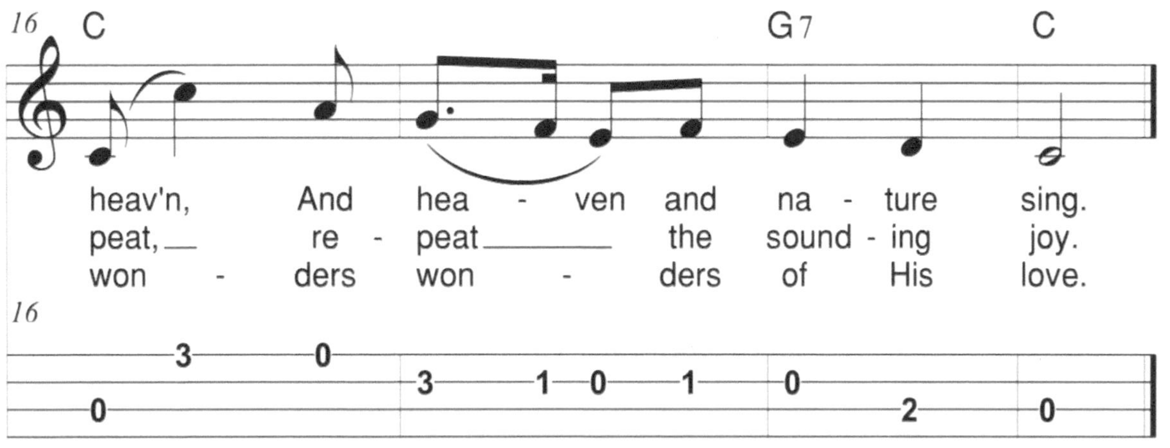

Four-Chord Holiday Songs

Our three four-chord songs, "Jolly Old St. Nicholas," "Deck the Halls" and "Auld Lang Syne" add only one new chord to the three you played in the songs of the last chapter: A minor. Fortunately, it's a very easy chord – it only uses one finger.

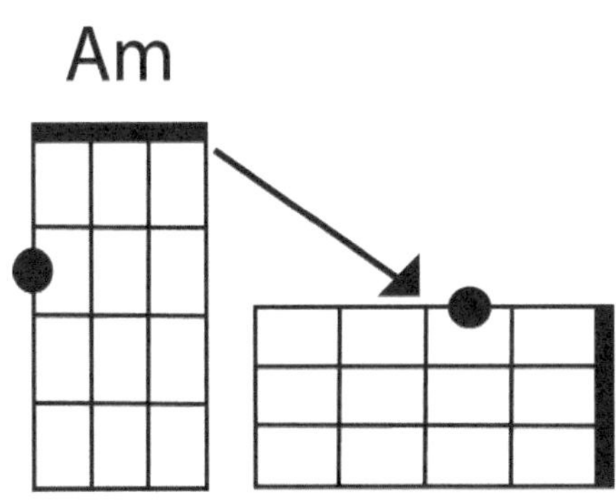

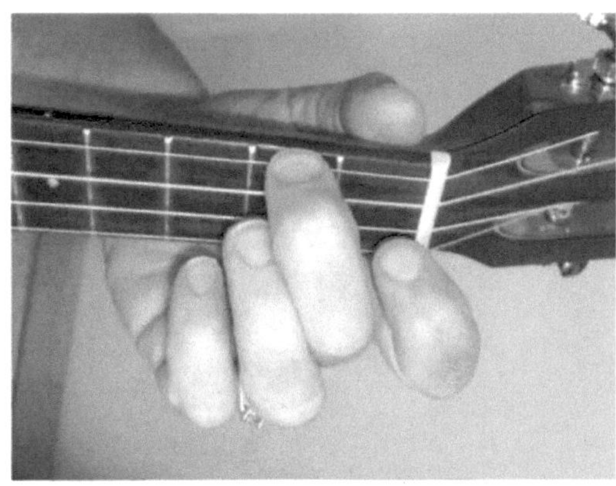

This page is intentionally left blank to avoid unnecessary page turns.

Jolly Old St. Nicholas

With its litany of Christmas wishes, this song about a whispered conference with Santa Claus is a children's favorite. It's one of the few well-known Christmas songs with no known author. Its style hints that it was written in the mid-1800s, and some musical experts suspect that its author is Benjamin R. Hanby, who wrote "Up on the Housetop" around the same time. It's easy to make up new lyrics for children (or adults) who want to list their favorite toys. Try inserting "bag of ukes" instead of "pair of skates" or "picture book" in the second verse and see how it works out.

For this song we recommend doing Strum #1 when you are first learning it. Once you've got the hang of the lyrics and chords, you might try the more complicated strumming pattern of down, down-up-down, down-up-down. This is the same pattern that we suggested for "O Come Little Children" and "Up on the Housetop."

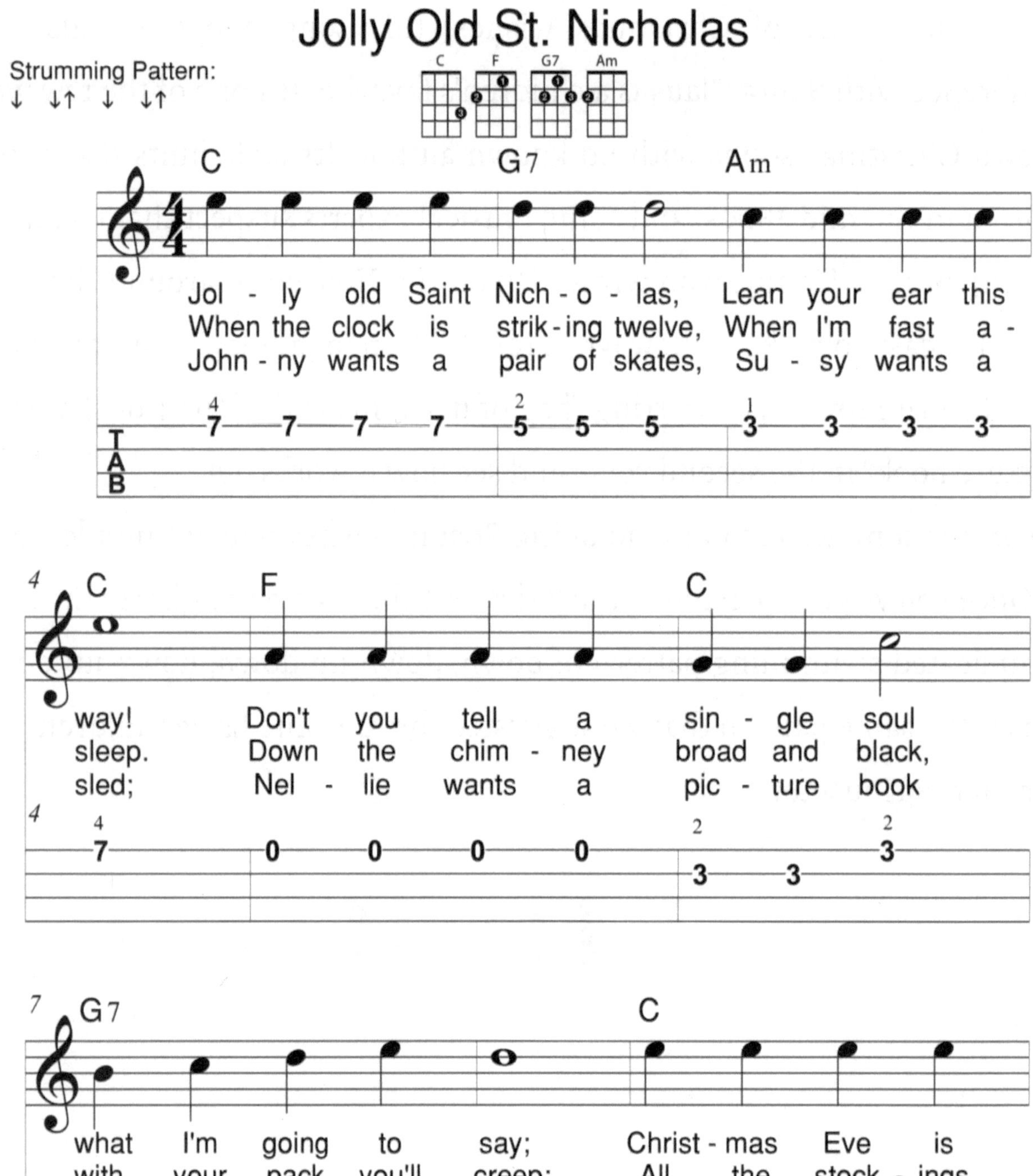
Jolly Old St. Nicholas
Strumming Pattern:
↓ ↓↑ ↓ ↓↑
C G7 Am
Jol - ly old Saint Nich - o - las, Lean your ear this
When the clock is strik - ing twelve, When I'm fast a -
John - ny wants a pair of skates, Su - sy wants a
C F C
way! Don't you tell a sin - gle soul
sleep. Down the chim - ney broad and black,
sled; Nel - lie wants a pic - ture book
G7 C
what I'm going to say; Christ - mas Eve is
with your pack you'll creep; All the stock - ings
Yel - low blue, and red; Now I think I'll

Jolly Old St. Nicholas 2

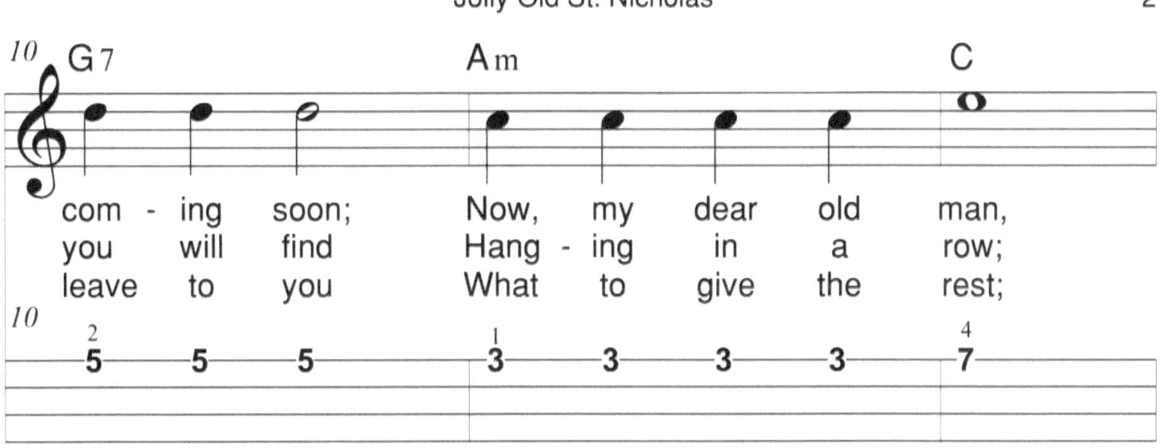

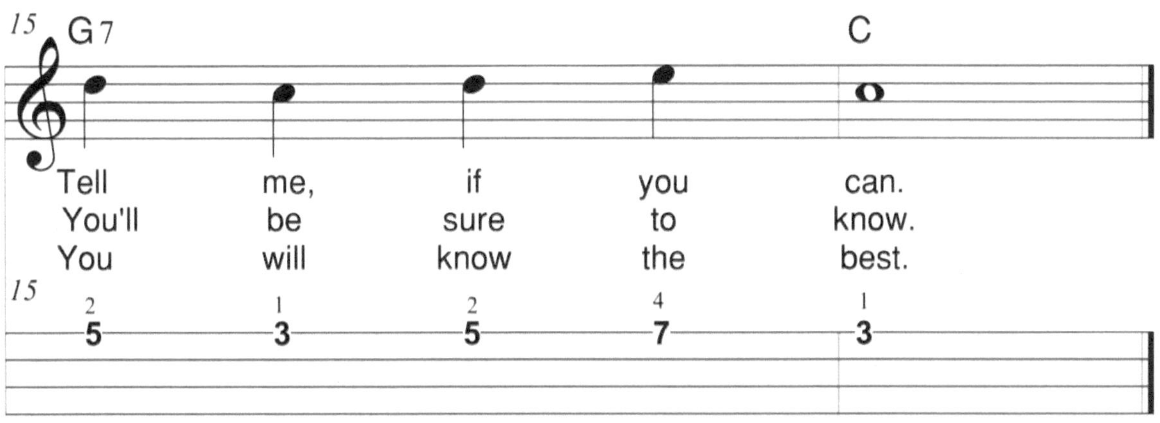

This page is intentionally left blank to avoid unnecessary page turns.

Deck the Halls

There's no hushed reverence in this song – it's all about Christmas partying! Although it's one of the most famous holiday carols, very little is known about its heritage. It probably originated in Wales, but the lyrics fit the music a bit too neatly to be a translation from the Welsh language. Guesses at when it was written range from the Middle Ages in Europe, to 1881 in New York City where it was first printed. Because it has the character of an English madrigal, it seems to fit best in the sixteenth century, Shakespeare's time. In fact, we suspect that the Bard himself was known to indulge in a bit of "fa la la la la"!

We suggest the same strums for "Deck the Halls" that we described for "Jolly Old Saint Nicholas." In case you think we have run short on inspiration, the real reason we are suggesting the same strums again is that often songs that have the same rhythmic feel, or meter, sound good with the same strumming patterns. In the sheet music, the meter is shown by the ***time signature***, which is the two numbers aligned vertically over each other at the beginning of the song.

Deck the Halls

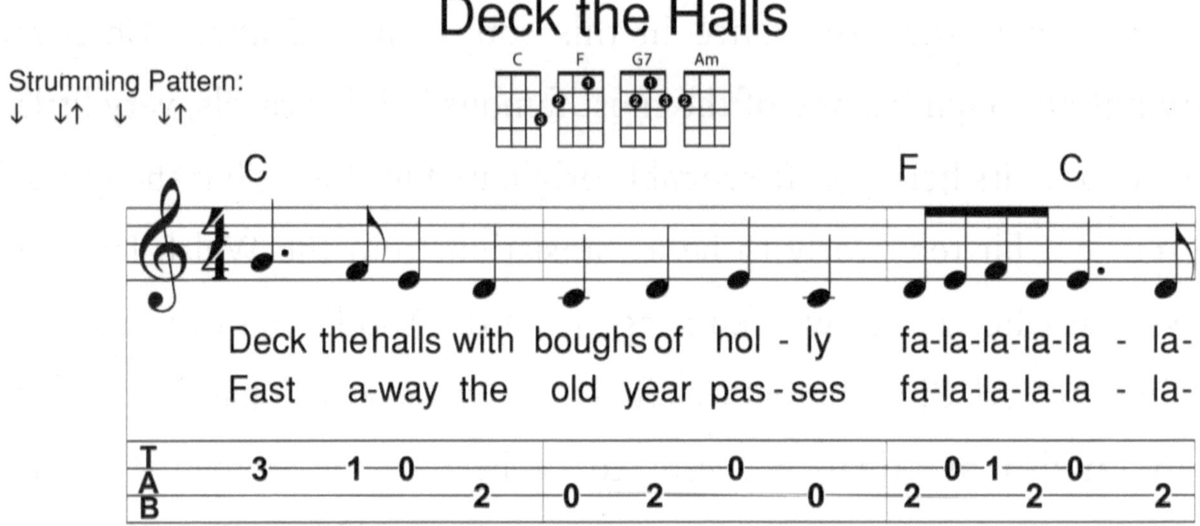

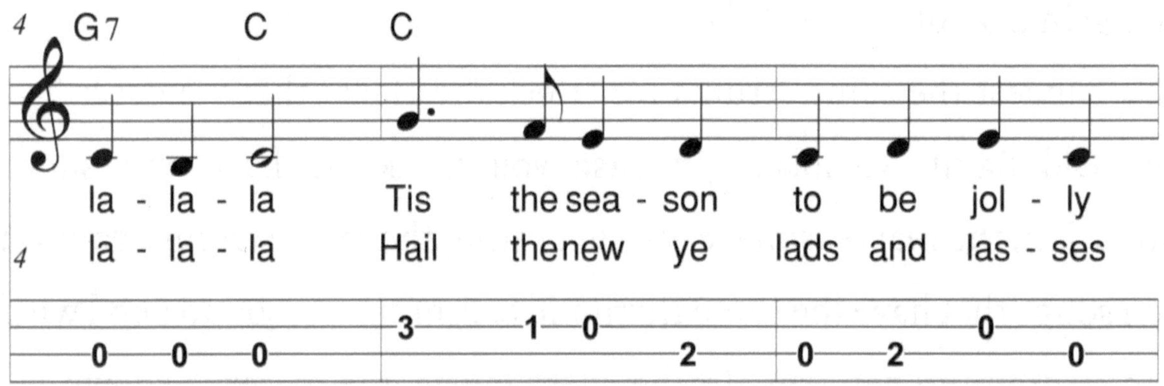

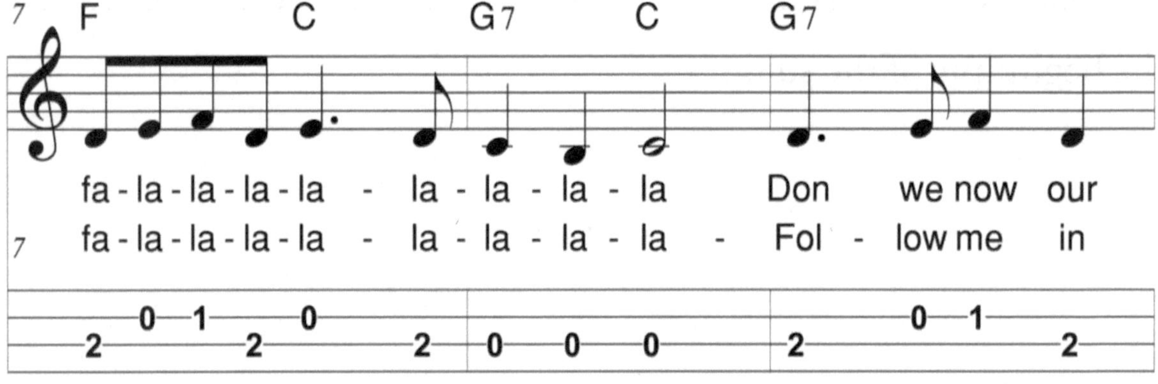

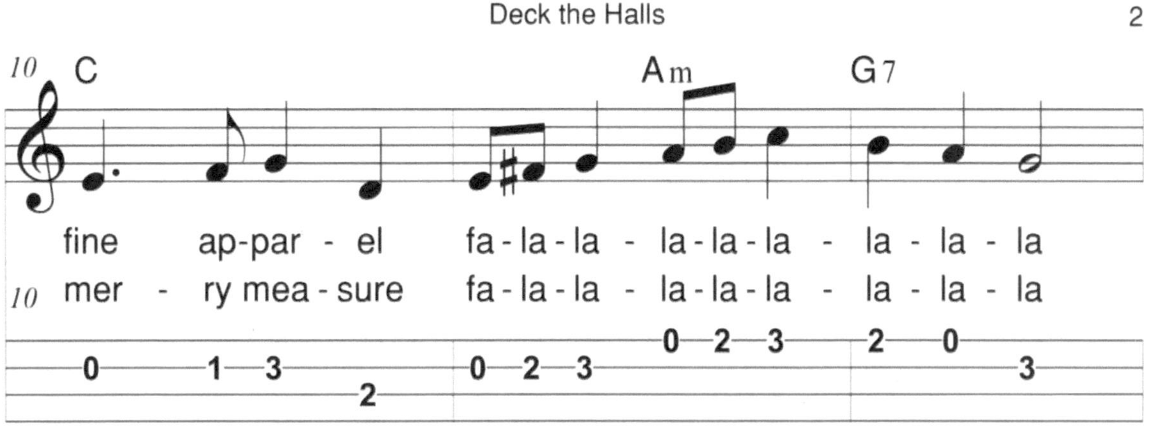
Deck the Halls
2
C
Am
G7
fine ap-par - el fa - la - la - la - la - la - la - la - la
mer - ry mea - sure fa - la - la - la - la - la - la - la - la

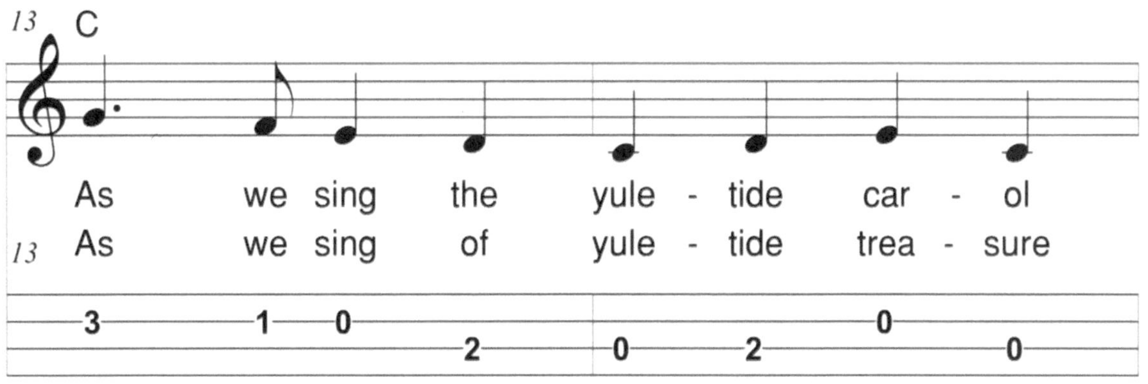
C
As we sing the yule - tide car - ol
As we sing of yule - tide trea - sure

F
C
G7
C
fa - la - la - la - la - la - la - la - la
fa - la - la - la - la - la - la - la - la

This page is intentionally left blank to avoid unnecessary page turns.

Auld Lang Syne

Everyone knows and sings this classic New Year's song. Its heritage is Scottish and translated from its Scottish dialect the title means "old long since." Although its first verse predates the eighteenth century, the Scottish poet Robert Burns contributed the second and third verses in 1788, so he often gets credit for writing the entire song. In reality it's much older than Burns, perhaps as old as the sixteenth century. "Auld Lang Syne" celebrates old times and the ringing in of the New Year.

Since this song is in the same meter as "Deck the Halls" and "Up on the Housetop," choose either all down strums, or the more ornate down, down-up-down, down-up-down pattern that we recommended for these songs earlier in this book. "Auld Lang Syne" is played at a slow ***tempo***, so it's a good choice for learning to play with up strums. This song is another one that sounds good with fingerpicked chords. Since it is in 4/4 time, you would use the same pattern of plucking described in "Good King Wenceslas": pluck the outer two strings once and the inner two strings once.

We've made an easier version of this song with only four chords. In the video, Jenny adds an optional E7 chord in measures 7 and 15, shown in parentheses in the sheet music. Feel free to leave out this quick chord change if it is difficult for you.

Auld Lang Syne

Strumming Pattern:
↓ ↓↑ ↑↓↑

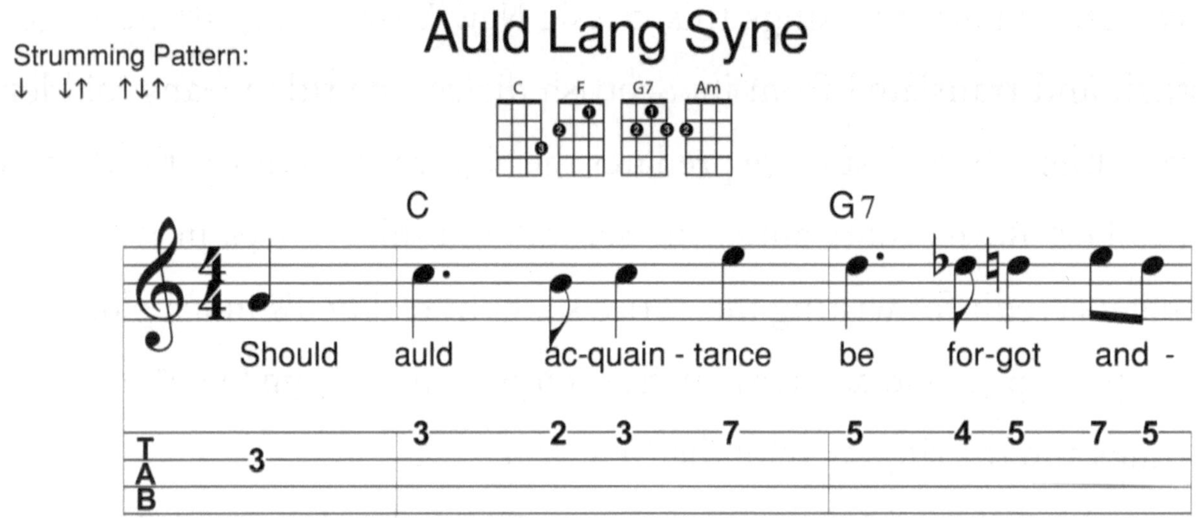

Auld Lang Syne 2

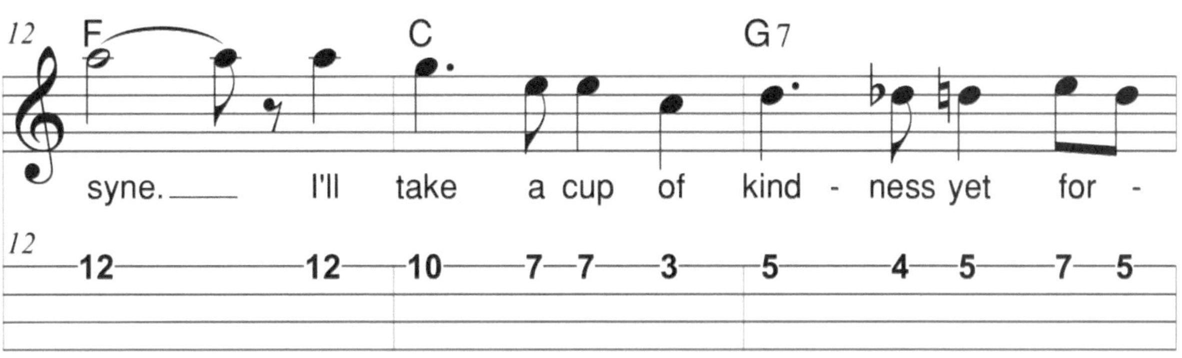

Minor Mode

Three New Chords

To tackle the next group of songs, you'll have to learn three additional chords.

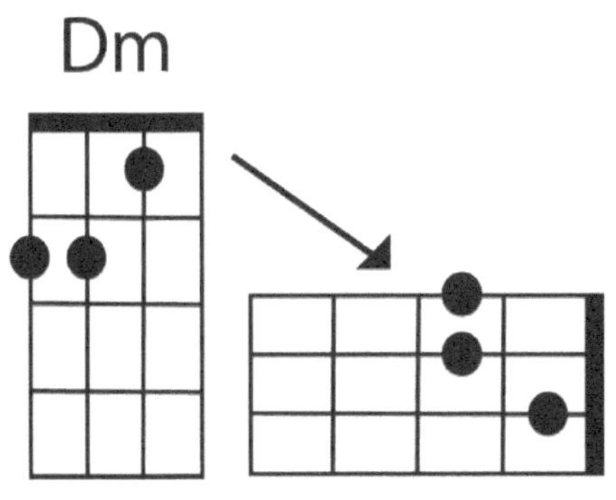

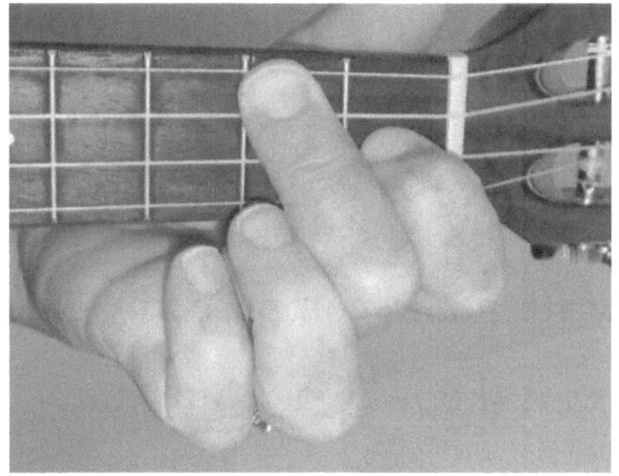

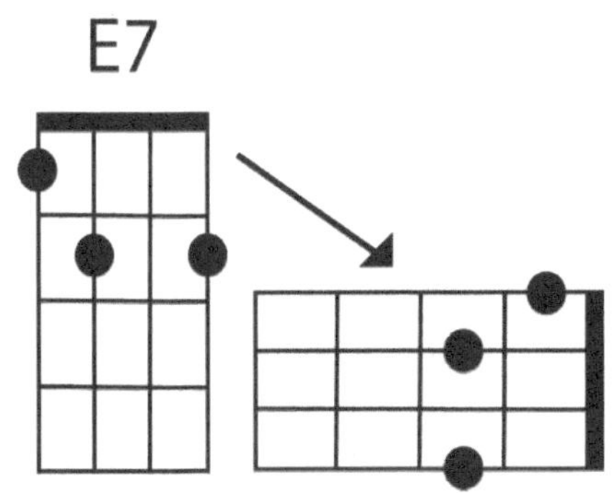

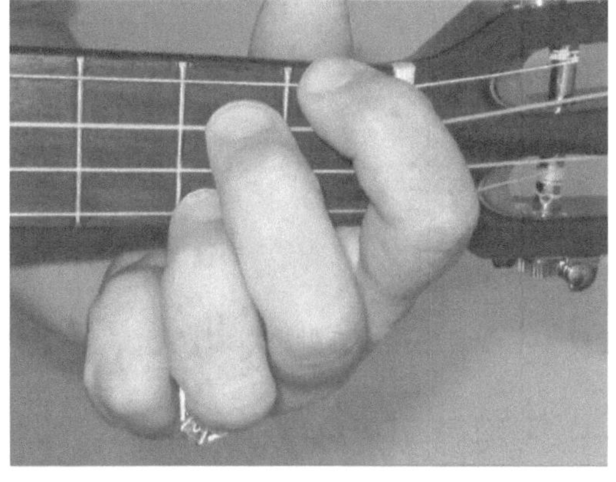

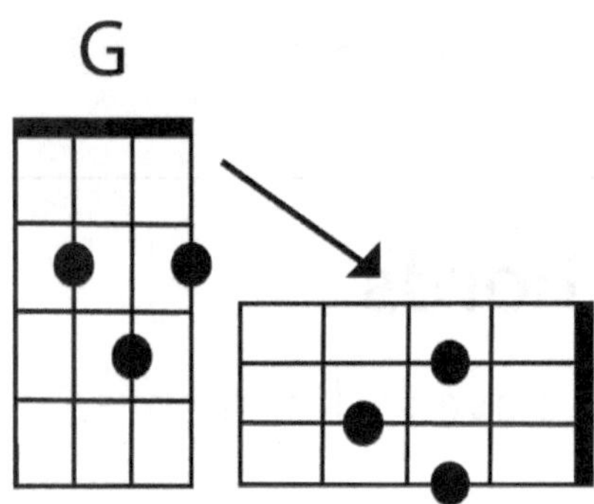

Patapan

This musical message to "the little drummer boy" was written long before the later song with that title. It hails from the Burgundy region of France and was written and composed by Bernard de la Monnoye around 1700. While most of us know about Burgundy because of its wine, it's also a rich source of Christmas carols. In fact, Monnoye wrote a number of Christmas poems that are still in publication today. We love "Patapan" because of its brisk meter and its joyful message to Willie and his friends to celebrate Christmas with music.

If you keep in mind that the E7 chord is shaped like the G7 chord it will be easier to learn. Take your time learning to play the D minor chord. It's shaped like an F major chord, but you have to collapse the knuckle of your middle finger to stop both the third and fourth strings at the same time.

Practice changing back and forth between F and D minor until your second finger easily drops into the collapsed position.

You can simplify the process of learning this song by practicing these two-chord progressions:

- Am to E7 to Am
- Am to Dm to E7 to Am

Once you are good at switching between these chord shapes, then go ahead and learn the melody, lyrics, and strumming pattern. Start with the easy pattern of one down strum per beat and put a strong accent on each down strum so it sounds like a drum. Another pattern that simulates a drumbeat is down, down-up-down, down-up-down. (This is the same pattern we suggested for "O Come Little Children," "Jolly Old Saint Nicholas" and "Up on the Housetop.")

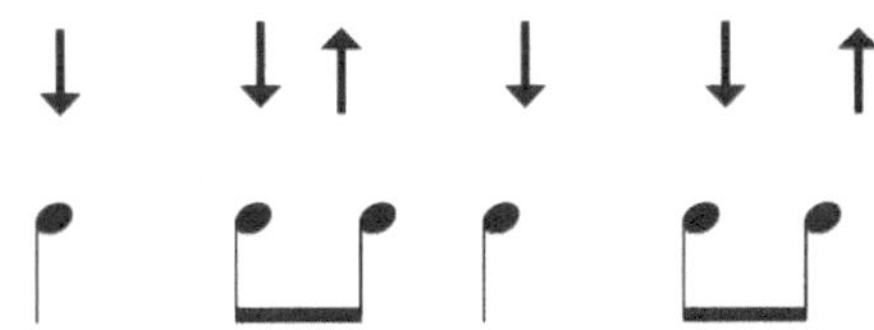

Patapan
Strumming Pattern:
↓ ↓↑ ↓ ↓↑
Am E7 Dm
Am E7 Am E7
Wil - lie, take your lit - tle drum, Ro - bin take your
When the men of old - en days gave the King of
God and man this day be - come joined as one with
T
A
B
3 Am E7
flute and come, When we hear the tune you
Kings their praise, They had pipes on which to
pipe and drum, Let the hap - py tune play
6 Am Dm E7
play, Tu - re - lu - re - lu, pat - a - pat - a - pan; When we
play, Tu - re - lu - re - lu, pat - a - pat - a - pan; They had
on, Tu - re - lu - re - lu, pat - a - pat - a - pan; Flute and

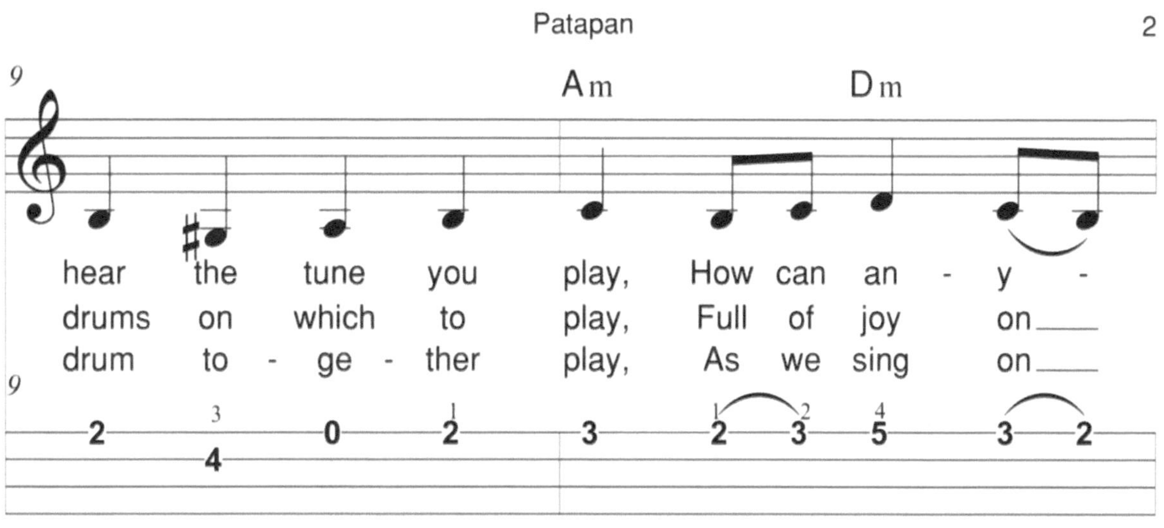
Patapan
2
9
Am
Dm
hear the tune you play, How can an - y -
drums on which to play, Full of joy on
drum to - ge - ther play, As we sing on
9
2 3 4 0 1 2 3 1 2 2 3 4 5 3 2

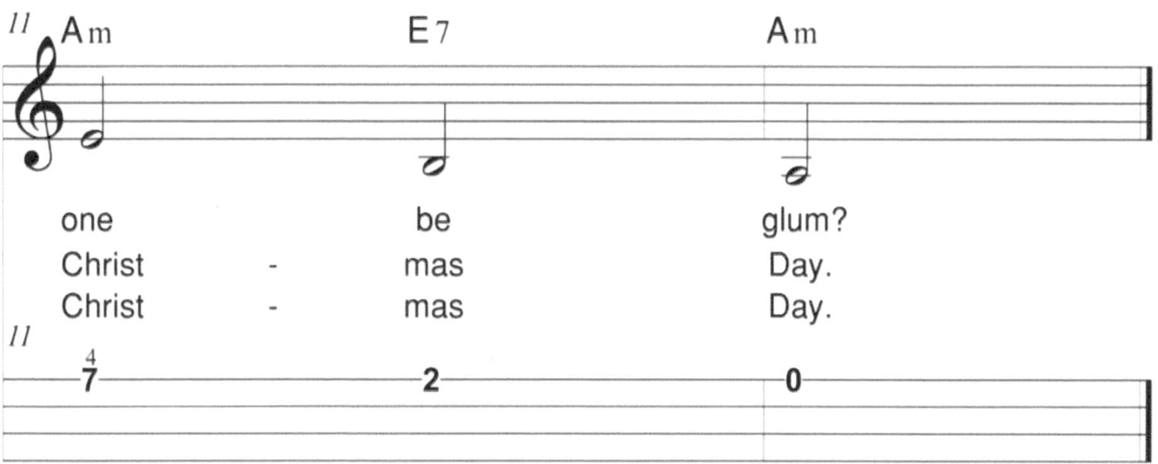
11
Am
E7
Am
one be glum?
Christ - mas Day.
Christ - mas Day.
11
4 7 2 0

This page is intentionally left blank to avoid unnecessary page turns.

We Three Kings of Orient Are

The American Episcopal clergyman John Henry Hopkins, Jr., wrote this carol about the Three Wise Men to delight his nieces and nephews on a family Christmas visit to Vermont in 1857. Although the biblical Magi (Wise Men) in Matthew Chapter 2 weren't exactly kings and their country of origin is unclear, the song tells a colorful story about their great journey as they followed the star of Bethlehem westward. We suspect that "Uncle Henry" was a master storyteller – at least on family holidays!

The contrast between the verse and chorus of this song makes it more interesting. It starts out with the minor chord progression of A minor to D minor to E7 and back to A minor. It then shifts to major chords as it glowingly describes the "star of wonder" in the chorus.

In the video, Rebecca uses a very easy strum – only one down strum per measure – in order to concentrate on the chord changes. Jenny varies her strumming patterns between verse and chorus. She begins with down, down-up, down for the verse and down-up, down-up, down-up for the chorus – definitely for more advanced players.

We Three Kings of Orient Are

Strumming Pattern:
↓ ↓↑ ↓

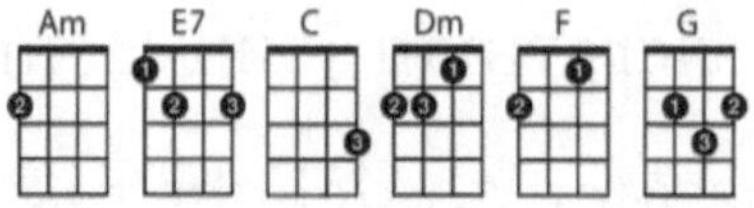

Am E7

We three kings of Or - i - ent
Born a king on Beth - le - hem's
Fran - kin - cense to of - fer have

7 5 3 0 2 3 2

4 Am

are; bear - ing gifts we
plain, gold I bring to
I; In - cense owns a

0 7 5 3 0

7 E7 Am C

tra - verse a - far. Field and
crown him a - gain. King for -
De - i - ty nigh; prayer and

2 3 2 0 3 3

10 G Am F

foun - tain, moor and mount - tain
e - ver, ceas - ing ne___ ver,
prais - ing voic - es rais - ing,

5 5 7 7 10 8 7

We Three Kings of Orient Are 2

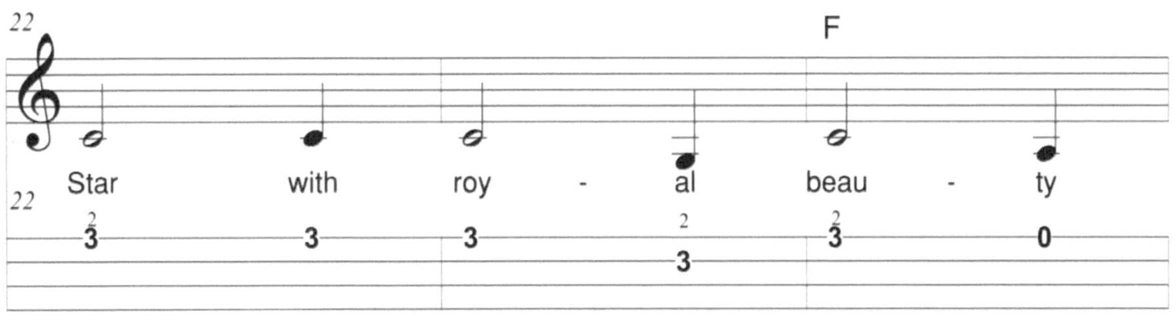

3 We Three Kings of Orient Are

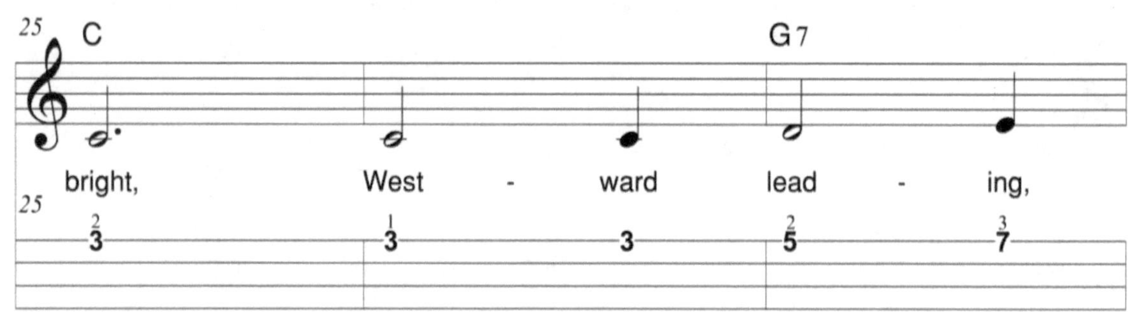

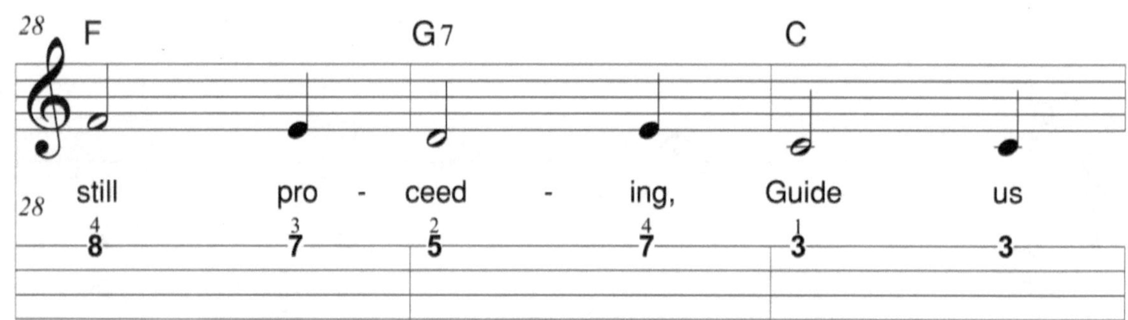

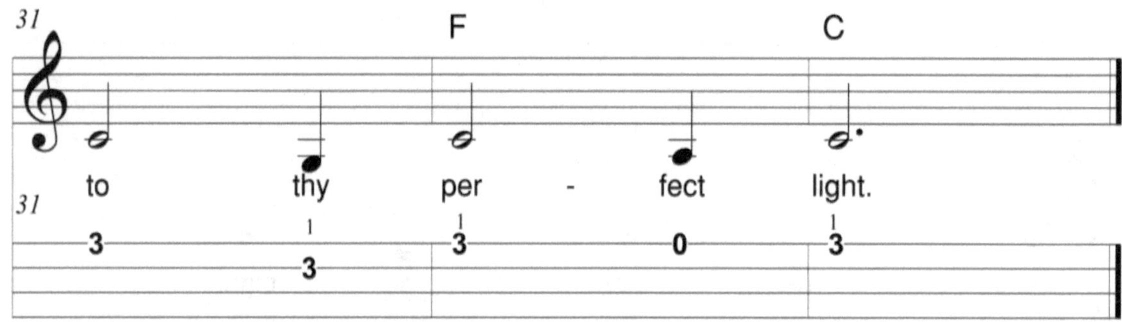

What Child Is This?

Set to the music of the sixteenth-century love song, "Greensleeves," this delicate Christmas carol is a delight to play and sing. The author of "Greensleeves" is unknown, although King Henry VIII of England claimed credit for writing it for one of his six wives. In reality it was probably written in the Elizabethan era, and in fact Shakespeare mentions it in one of his plays. The Christmas lyrics were written in 1865 by English poet William Chatterton Dix. If you switch over to the "Greensleeves" lyrics after the holidays are over, you can play it all year long.

We also add a fingerpicked version of the chords, to give this song a medieval flavor. Practice changing from A minor to G and back to A minor until this difficult chord progression becomes second nature.

The song is in 3/4 time, so you can play a pattern of three down strums per measure, or the more challenging down, down-up, down strumming pattern. To make a great sounding fingerpicked accompaniment, begin by plucking the outer two strings. Then pluck the inner strings twice in a row before going back to plucking the outer strings. Your left hand would continue to make the same chord shapes that you make when you are strumming. Keep track by chanting, "out, out, in, in, in, in."

What Child is This?
Strumming Pattern
↓ ↓↑ ↓
Am G C E7 F
English Folk Song
Arr. Jenny Peters
What child is this, who laid to rest, on Mary's lap is sleeping? Whom angels greet with anthems sweet, while shepherds watch are keep-
Oh. bring Him incense, gold and myrrh, Come peasant, king to own Him; The King of kings salvation brings, Let loving hearts enthrone

What Child is This?
2
CHORUS
C G
ing? This, this is Christ the
Him. Raise, raise the song on
Am E7
King; whom shep - herds guard and an - gels
high, the vir - gin sings a lul - la -
C G
sing; Haste, haste to bring Him
by. Haste, haste to bring Him
Am E7 Am
laud, the Babe the Son of Ma - ry.
laud, the Babe the Son of Ma - ry.

Am G E7 C F

What Child Is This?

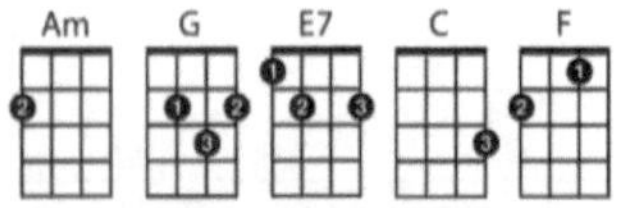

Finger Picking Accompaniment

Am

What child is this, who
So bring Him in - cense,

Am

3 G F

laid to rest, on Ma - ry's
gold and myrrh, Come pea - sant,

3

3 G F

6 E7

lap is sleep - ing? Whom
king to own Him; The

6

6 E7

What Child Is This?
2
Am
G
an - gels greet with an - thems
King of kings sal - va - tion
Am
G
Am
E7
sweet, while shep - herds watch are
brings, Let lov - ing hearts en -
Am
E7
CHORUS
Am
C
keep - - - ing? This,
throne Him. Raise,
Am
C

3 What Child Is This?

What Child Is This?
4
27
G
Am
bring Him laud, the Babe the
bring Him laud, the Babe the
30
E7
Am
Son of Ma - - - ry.
Son of Ma - - - ry.

This page is intentionally left blank to avoid unnecessary page turns.

God Rest Ye Merry, Gentlemen

Not just another Christmas carol, this song is the carol that provided the title for Dickens' famous Christmas story. Early in "A Christmas Carol," a street child approaches Scrooge and quotes the first two lines of this song before the old man chases him away. Shortly afterward, Scrooge is given plenty of things to be dismayed about. The song itself probably predates Dickens by a few centuries. Its words and rhythm strongly resemble the style of Shakespeare's time, which would put it in the sixteenth century. The author, however, remains unknown.

This song also uses the D minor chord, so make sure you're comfortable collapsing the knuckle of your middle finger to stop both the third and fourth strings at once. Fortunately, A7 and C7 are both one-finger chords to keep things simple. There's also a C chord thrown in to keep you on your toes.

Practice the following chord changes:

- Dm to A7 to Dm
- F to C7 to F

You can start out with all down strums and progress to the down, down-up-down, down-up-down pattern as you get better at the chord changes. Be sure try out the solo part in tab. It has no position shifts, so it's easy to learn.

God Rest Ye Merry, Gentlemen

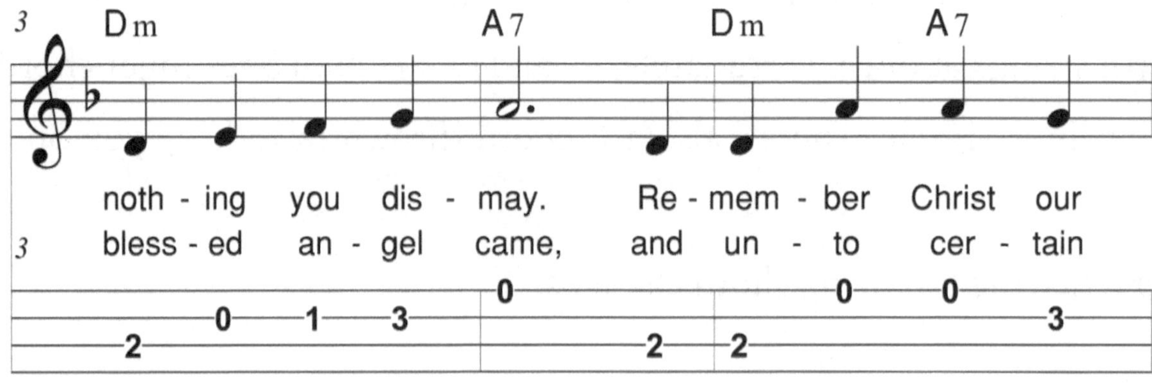

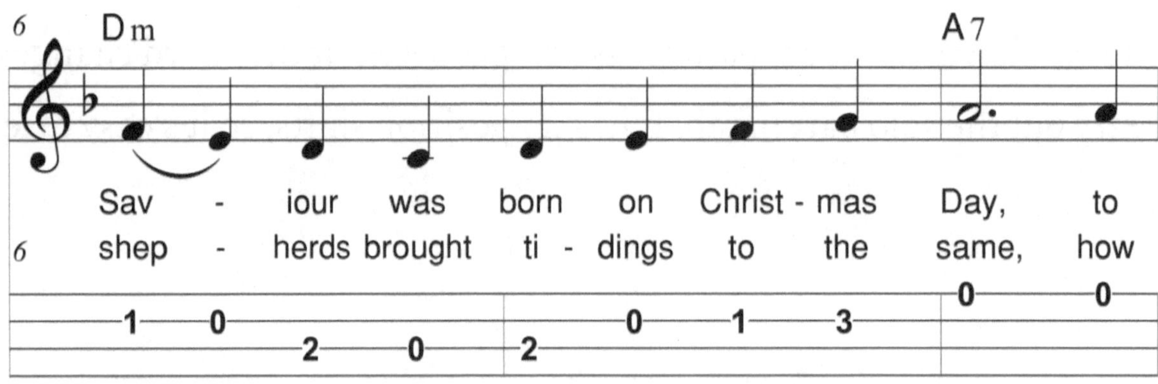

God Rest Ye Merry, Gentlemen
2
C7 F Dm
save us all from Sa - tan's pow'r when we were gone a
that in Beth - le - hem was born the Son of God by
C F A7
stray. Oh ti - dings of com - fort and
name,
Dm C F
joy, com-fort and joy, o - ti - dings of
A7 Dm
com - fort and joy.

Holiday Songs with 5 to 7 Chords

The songs in this section are more complicated. You will need to learn the D7 chord. We show two ways to play the D7 chord below. The top version of D7 is much easier because it only uses two fingers. Using the two-finger version of D7 makes it much easier to switch to the three finger G chord which often occurs right after the D7 in music because the D7 shape is closely related to the G shape. We both use the two finger D7 chord shape in the lesson videos.

Using the second version of D7 requires you to flatten your first finger in the second fret so you are stopping three strings with one finger. It can take quite a bit of practice to get comfortable with this flattened finger position, which is referred to as a ***barre*** (or "bar"). The big plus with using the D7 barre chord shape is that you can then slide your left hand up and down the fret board and play lots of other similar sounding chords using the same hand shape. Ukulele players refer to this type of chord as a movable barre chord.

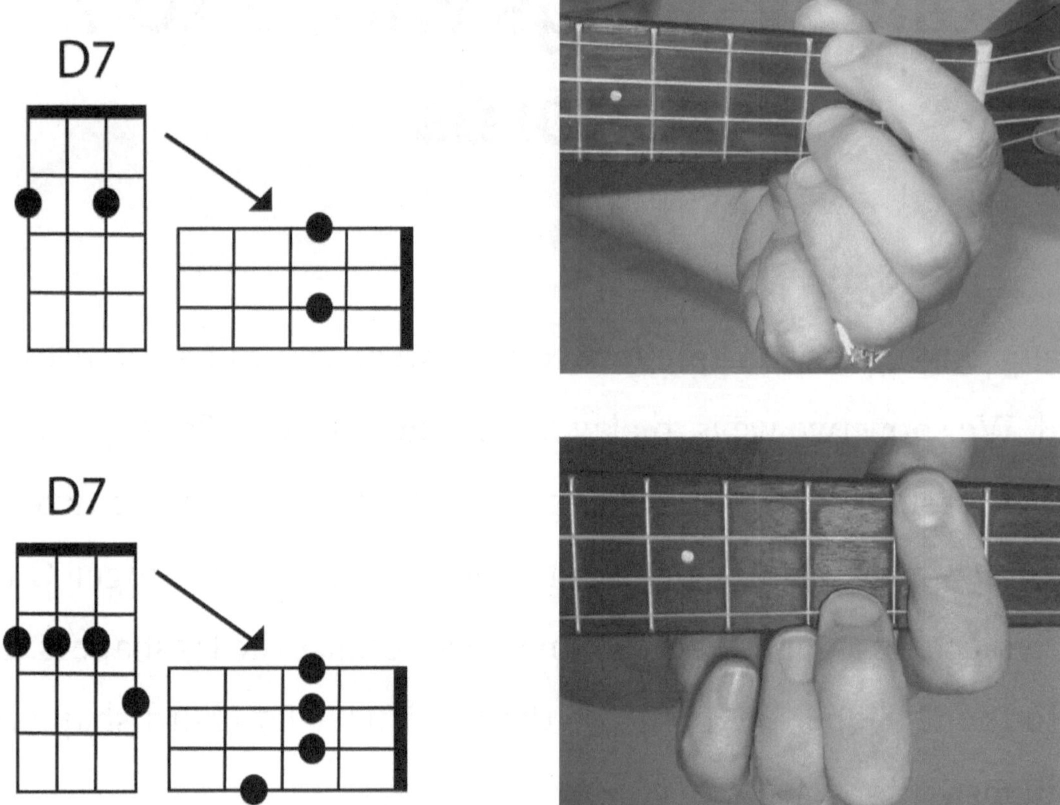

We also show some more complicated strumming patterns. But it's perfectly fine to learn the songs first with a simple down, down, down pattern and then spice up your strumming later.

O Come All Ye Faithful

This stately carol is translated from the Latin original, "Adeste Fidelis." The English Roman Catholic priest, John Francis Wade, wrote it around 1750 while living at the Catholic college for Englishmen in Douai, France. It is truly an international carol – written in Latin by an Englishman living at a French institution built by King Philip of Spain and carried around the world by the Portuguese. Written as a processional (announcing the beginning of a religious service), the melody is classical in every sense of the word.

We won't mince words – the chord changes in this song are not easy! For the D7, use the easy one with only two fingers, and practice switching between D7 to G and back to D7. Try shifting both fingers down one string toward the floor at the same time and then adding your ring finger afterward. With practice you'll be able to do this as one motion.

As you learn this song, imagine a steady marching rhythm, like the wedding march ("Here Comes the Bride"). A simple down strum on each beat is an easy place to start with "O Come All Ye Faithful," with an even down-up, down-up, down-up, down-up pattern added later as you get better at the chord changes. Strum softly so you can hear the vocal part.

O Come All Ye Faithful

O Come All Ye Faithful 

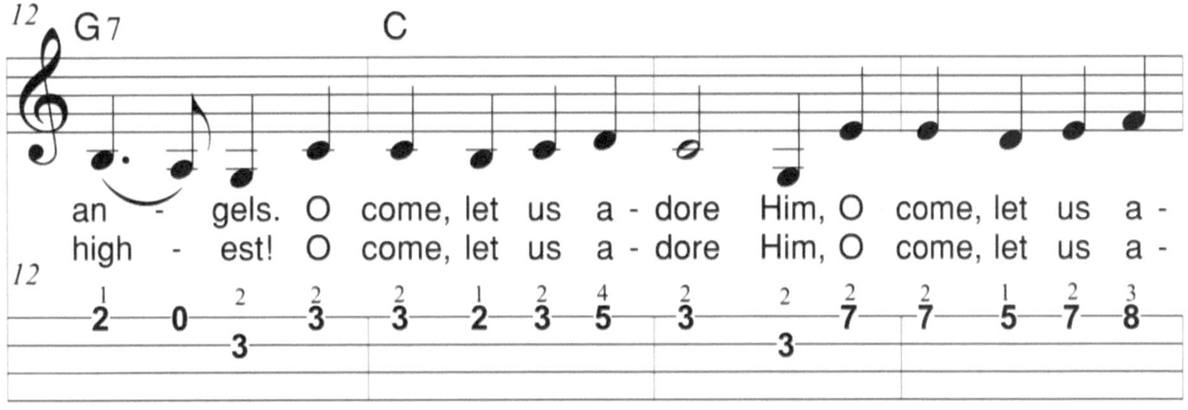

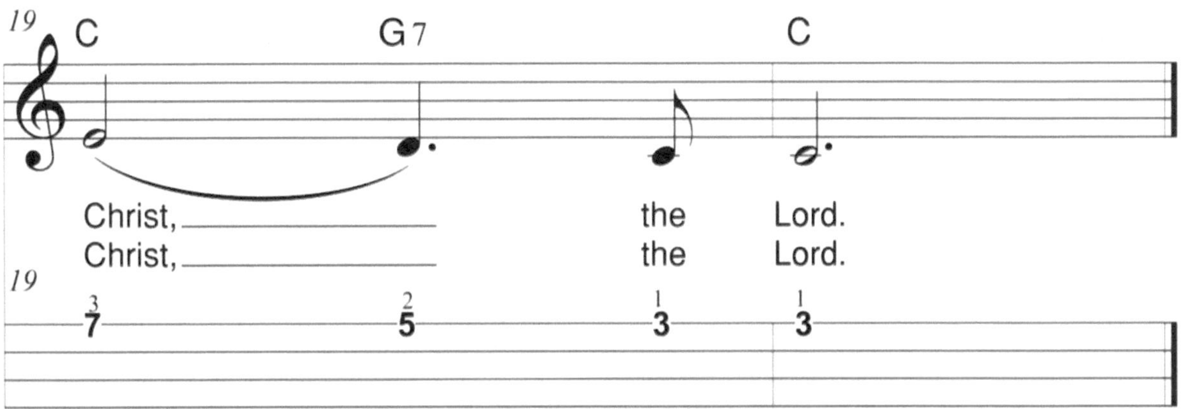

This page is intentionally left blank to avoid unnecessary page turns.

Hark the Herald Angels Sing

This Christmas carol dates to the time of Charles and John Wesley, brothers who co-founded the Methodist Church in England in the 1700s. Charles wrote the lyrics, which John then published in a book of religious poems in 1739. In 1855, William Hayman Cummings, an English organist, set "Hark!" to music. Cummings was a fan of Felix Mendelssohn and chose a little-known snippet from the great German classical composer's work to match with the Wesleys' poem.

If you've mastered the songs presented so far, then the six chords in this song probably won't faze you. Use the easier two-fingered version of D7 and practice the G to D7 to G progression until you can move all three of your fingers smoothly from one set of strings to the other and back again. Remember to collapse the knuckle of your middle finger to stop both the third and fourth strings at once for the D minor chord.

The strumming pattern for this song is down-up, down-up, down-up, down-up, or Strum #2, but of course you can start out with the simpler pattern of four down strums until you dial in the chord changes.

Hark! the Herald Angels Sing

Strumming Pattern:
↓↑↓↑↓↑↓↑

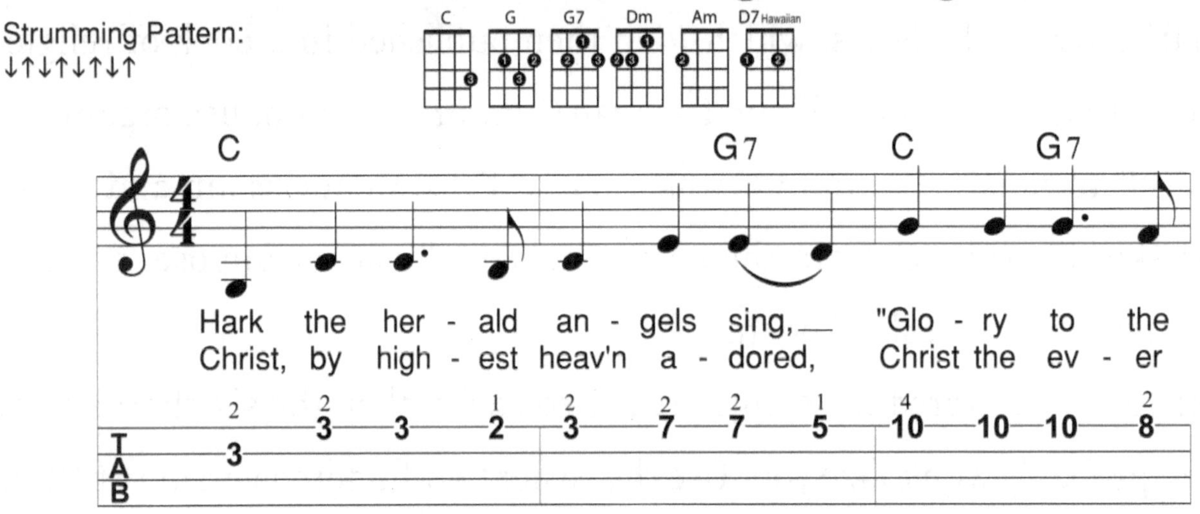

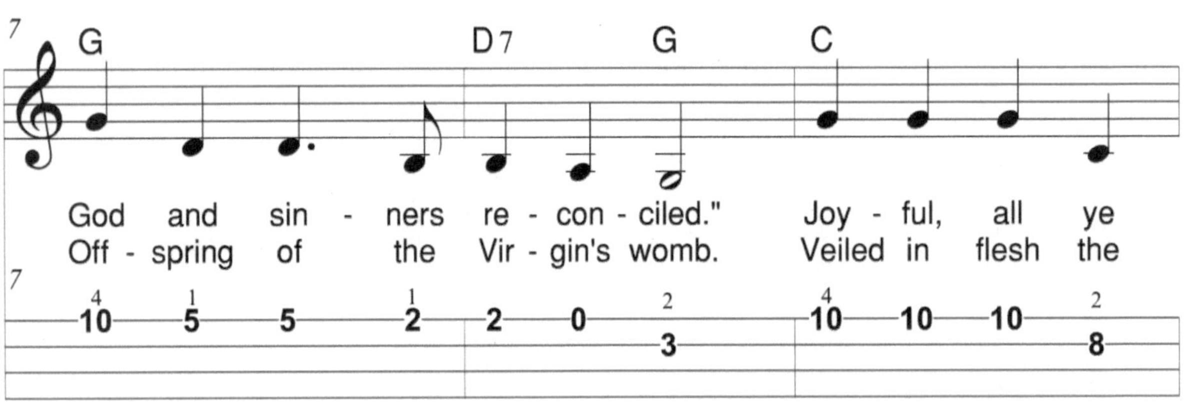

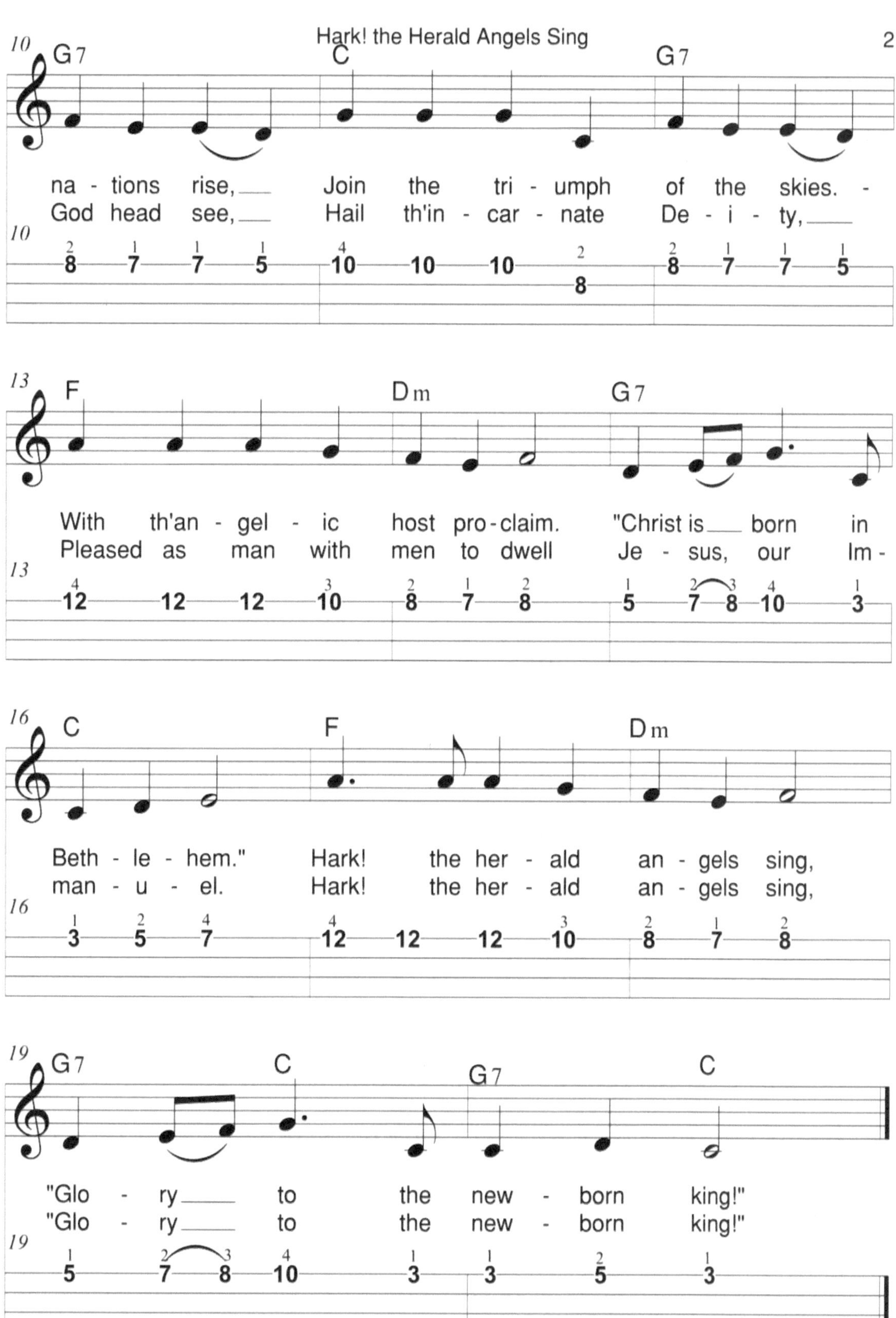
Hark! the Herald Angels Sing
2
G7 C G7
na - tions rise, Join the tri - umph of the skies. -
God head see, Hail th'in - car - nate De - i - ty,
F Dm G7
With th'an - gel - ic host pro-claim. "Christ is born in
Pleased as man with men to dwell Je - sus, our Im -
C F Dm
Beth - le - hem." Hark! the her - ald an - gels sing,
man - u - el. Hark! the her - ald an - gels sing,
G7 C G7 C
"Glo - ry to the new - born king!"
"Glo - ry to the new - born king!"

The Twelve Days of Christmas

"Counting songs" are common in children's music – for example, "Old McDonald Had a Farm" – but "The Twelve Days of Christmas" has an unusual pedigree. The lyrics are from English folklore, probably around the end of the seventeenth century, with charming images of leaping lords and swimming swans. The melody is another story. Since the song was published in England around 1780, the melody was also assumed to be English. However, there's a French folk tune with a nearly identical melody, so "Twelve Days" could easily be a musical hybrid from two countries who don't always get along.

It's fun to get silly with this song – in fact, it's almost impossible to get *too* silly with it, so don't be afraid to write your own lyrics, change the tempo, and have different people sing different verses.

Be sure you practice the "partridge in a pear tree" chord progression until you can do it quite quickly. The chords are C, F, C, G7, C, with one chord per beat. See how Jenny demonstrates this in the video. This song changes both tempo and key more and more as verses are added. The "four calling birds, three French hens" part is in 3/4 time, so a single down strum for each measure of these verses sounds great. For the 4/4 parts ("two turtle doves and a partridge in a pear tree"), play down, down-up, down, down-up, or you can just keep it simple and play all down strums. Days 6-12 are in 3/4 time and can be played with all down strums, or down, down-up, down.

The “five golden rings” verse temporarily changes to the key of G major, so it deserves a bit of special treatment. You can substitute the two-fingered form of D7 in place of the three-finger D chord if you wish. It’s fun to strum a tremolo for “rings” by quickly swinging your right index finger back and forth in the middle of the fretboard.

The Twelve Days of Christmas

The Twelve Days of Christmas
2
G C F C G7
three French hens, two tur-tle doves and a par-tridge in a pear
C C Am G7 C
tree. On the fourth day of Christ-mas, my true love sent to me
G
four call-ing birds, three French hens, two tur-tle doves, and a
C F C G7 C C Am
par-tridge in a pear tree. On the fifth day of Christ-mas, my

3
The Twelve Days of Christmas
G7 C G D7 G
true love sent to me Five gold - en rings,
C F
Four ___ call - ing birds, three French hens,
G7 C F C G7 C
two ___ tur - tledoves, and a par - tridge in a pear tree. On the
Am G7 C
sixth day of Christ - mas my true love sent to me
seventh day of Christ - mas my true love sent to me
eighth day of Christ - mas my true love sent to me
ninth day of Christ - mas my true love sent to me
tenth day of Christ - mas my true love sent to me
eleventh day of Christ - mas my true love sent to me
twelfth day of Christ - mas my true love sent to me

The Twelve Days of Christmas
4
G
G D7 G
six geese a lay - ing. Five gold-en rings,
seven swans a swim - ming,
eight maids a milk - ing,
nine la - dies danc - ing
ten lords a leap - ing
eleven pi - pers pip - ing,
twelve drum - mers drum - ming
C F G7
Four call - ing birds, three French hens, two tur - tle doves, and a
C F C G7 C 1. 2.
par - tridge in a pear tree. On the tree.

This page is intentionally left blank to avoid unnecessary page turns.

We Wish You a Merry Christmas

This little song feels light but carries a lot of weight. Practically everyone who celebrates Christmas has sung it at least once. It's old even by Christmas carol standards, with origins as a folk carol from the West Country of England, probably dating back to the sixteenth century. It's often sung to close out a Christmas concert or church pageant, despite its secular message. As its title suggests, it has a merry feeling and promotes good cheer and kinship as we celebrate the holidays.

This song is last because it's hard! It has seven chords, so you have an extra week to learn it. If you don't learn it by Christmas, you can still use your extra week and play it on New Year's. Practice the following chord progressions:

- G7 to C to G7
- D7 to G to D7

You can use the easy two-fingered version of D7 to make learning easier. There's also an E7 (which is similar to the G7), an A minor (which only requires one finger), and an F chord to keep you on your toes.

This song has a strong rhythm, so it sounds perfectly fine with all down strums. Once you've learned the chord changes, try adding an up strum on the second and fourth beats: down, down-up, down, down-up. The down-up on the fourth beat sounds especially good on the final words of the song as you sing "happy new year."

We Wish You a Merry Christmas

Strumming Pattern:
↓ ↓ ↓

We Wish You a Merry Christmas
2
G C F G7
kin, Good ti - dings for Christ - mas and a Hap - py New
C F D7
Year! We wish you a mer-ry Christ-mas, We wish you a mer-ry
G E7 Am
Christ - mas, We wish you a mer - ry Christ - mas and a
F G7 C
Hap - py New Year!

Enjoying This Book? You Can Make a Difference

Reviews are one of the most powerful marketing tools an author has. Honest reviews can help bring this book to the attention of other ukulele players who would benefit from it.

If you have enjoyed this book and found it helpful, Jenny and I would be very grateful if you could spend a few minutes leaving a short review on our book's Amazon page.

You can get there easily by typing ukulele.io/xmasreview-large into your browser window.

Thank you so much for your time and your help. We wish you a lifetime of happiness making music.

Rebecca Bogart and Jenny Peters

The Ukulele Sisters

How to Access Your Free Video Course at ukulele.io

You get a free video course because you bought this book. Follow the directions below or visit this page for a video and the most up-to-date instructions on how to access your course.

ukulele.io/access-free-video-course

Keeping our instructions up to date online instead of in print frees up time for us to create more books and courses for you. If you have any trouble, please drop us a note at ukulele.io/contact-us/. We want you to start enjoying your free course as soon as possible!

Here's What to Do

1. **Go to this secret link.**

ukulele.io/xmas

Or you can scan the QR Code on the following page:

2. You will see the page shown below. **Enter your email address in the box and click the green button** that says "Submit".

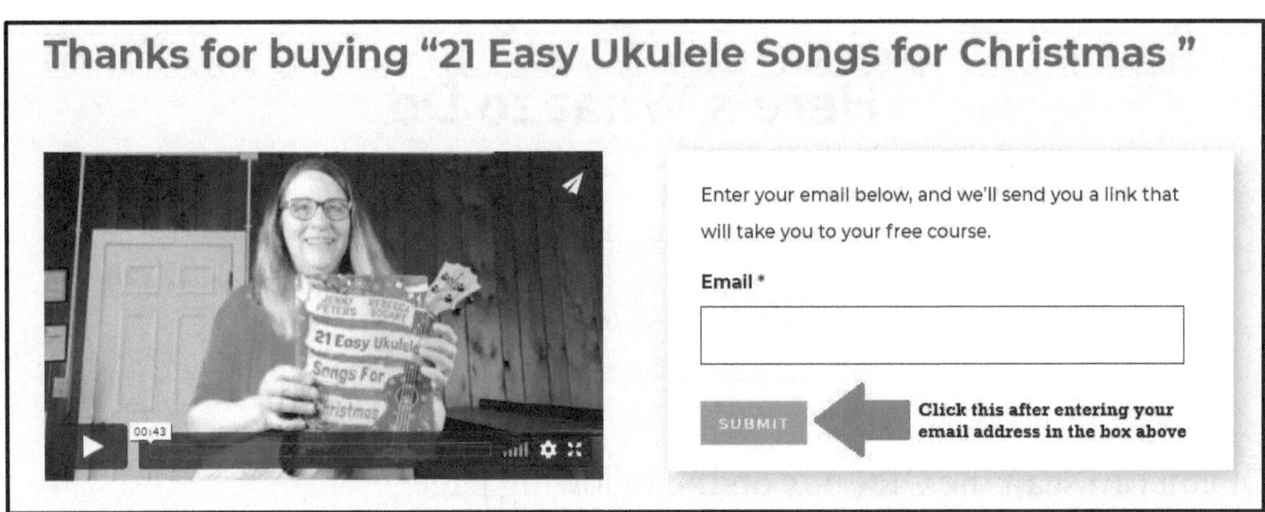

3. **Check your inbox** for an email from us. Click the link in the email. You'll be taken to a shopping cart in our store

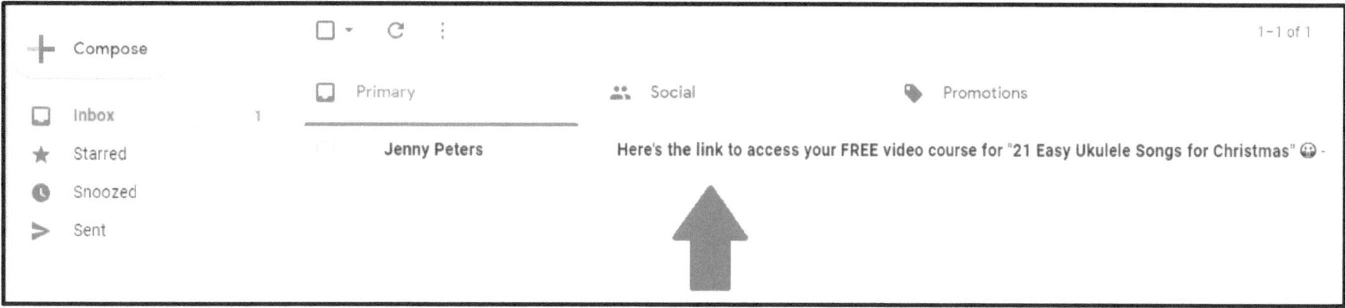

4. You'll see a video course in the cart discounted 100% so that you pay nothing. **Fill in the details under "Customer Information".** If you already have an account at ukulele.io, you'll need to log in first before placing your order.

If you have an existing account at ukulele.io and you clicked the "Click here to login" link, you'll see the following screen. Enter your username (or email) and password and click the "Login" button.

Once you've logged in (for returning customers) or entered the details under "Customer Information" (for new customers), scroll down and **click the green "Place Order Now" button**.

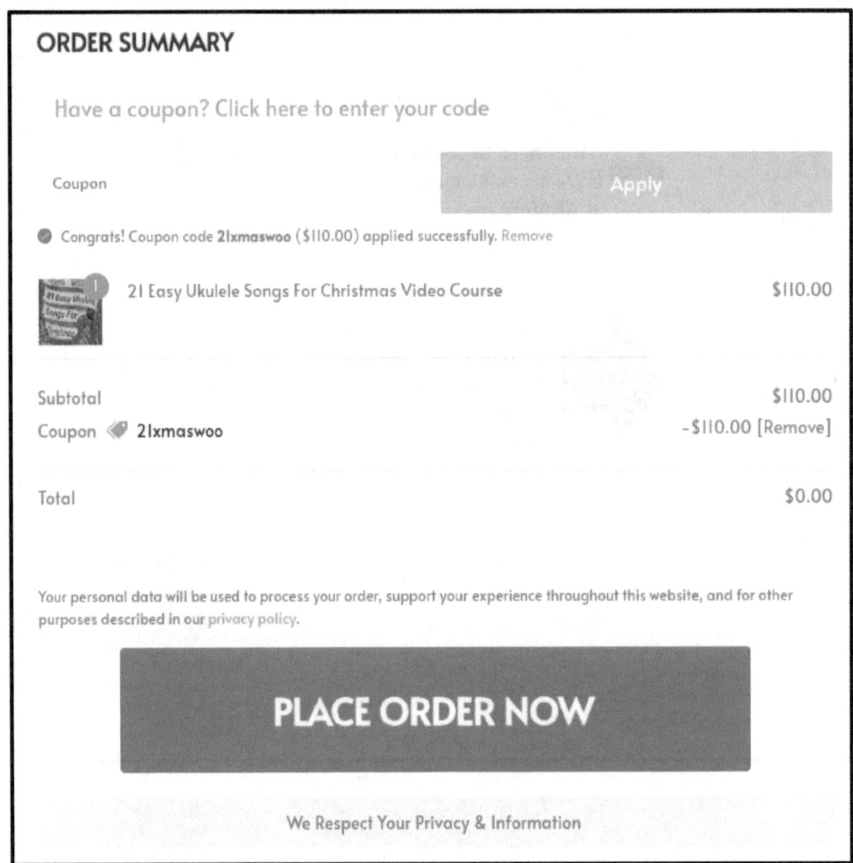

5. After you click "Place Order Now" you'll see this page. **Click on the link in the first line that says 'go to your courses page'.**

6. **Click on your course name to display the lesson names. Click on any lesson name to get to your course pages.** Enjoy!

Dashboard
Orders
My Membership
Subscriptions
Downloads
Payment methods
Account details
Courses
Log out

My Courses

Course	Progress	Overall Grade
▶ 21 Easy Ukulele Songs for Christmas	0%	N/A

7. **Check your email** for a message from us with your username and password so you can log in for later sessions. If you already have an account at ukulele.io, you will not receive an email with your username and password as you can continue to use your current username and password.

What If I Already Have an Account at ukulele.io?

Go ahead and enter your email at ukulele.io/xmas. Then go through each step above so that you 'purchase' the course that goes with this book using the 100% off coupon.

Just a heads up: you won't get an email from us with your username and password because you can use your current username and password. If you've forgotten your password, go to ukulele.io/my-account/ and click on 'Lost your password?' to reset your password.

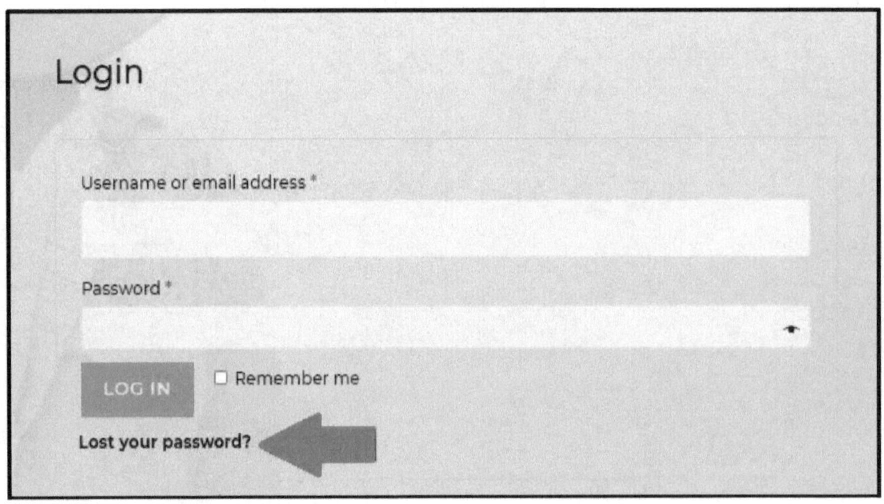

How to Sign In to Your Free Video Course at ukulele.io

Once you've signed up for your course using the secret link above, you can log in from the home page of ukulele.io for future practice sessions. Here's how.

1. Hover over "Sign In to Access Video Lessons" in the upper right corner of your screen. **Click on "My Account"** from the drop down menu that appears.

If you don't see the "Sign In" option, scroll right or enlarge your browser window until it appears. Or go directly to:

ukulele.io/my-account/

2. Enter your username and password. You will then be taken to this page. **Click on 'Courses'.**

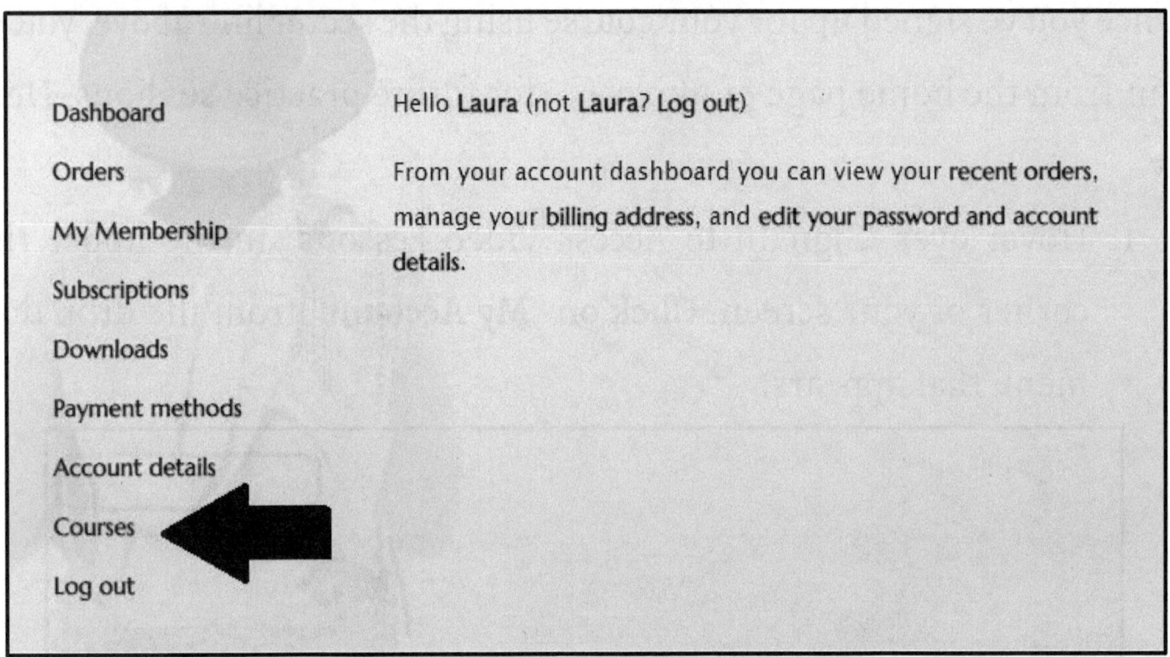

3. **Click on your course name** or the triangle in front of it. The names of the units will show up.

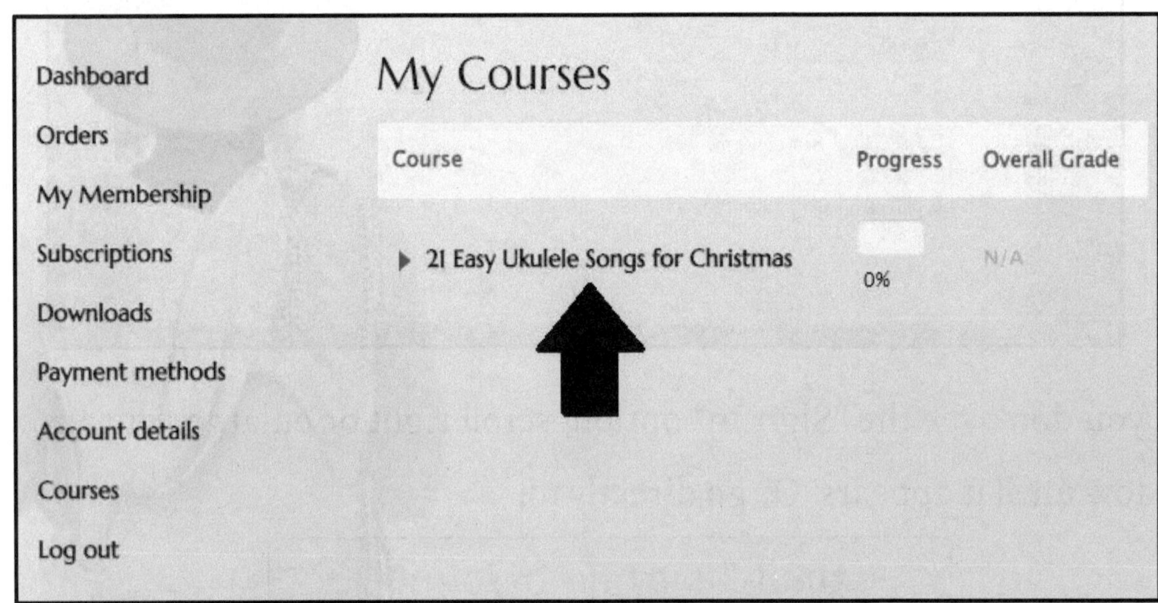

4. **Click on the lesson "Welcome: 21 Easy Ukulele Songs for Christmas" or any lesson name** to get to the lesson pages.

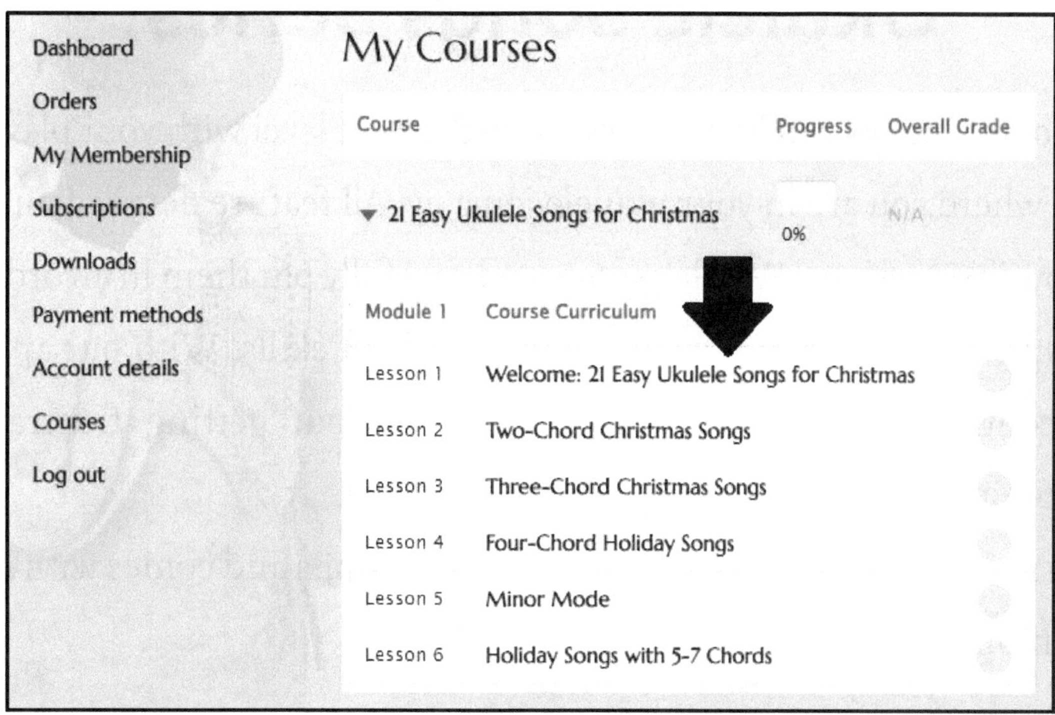

5. You will be taken to the following page. **Click on the left menu** to get to the lesson or course you want.

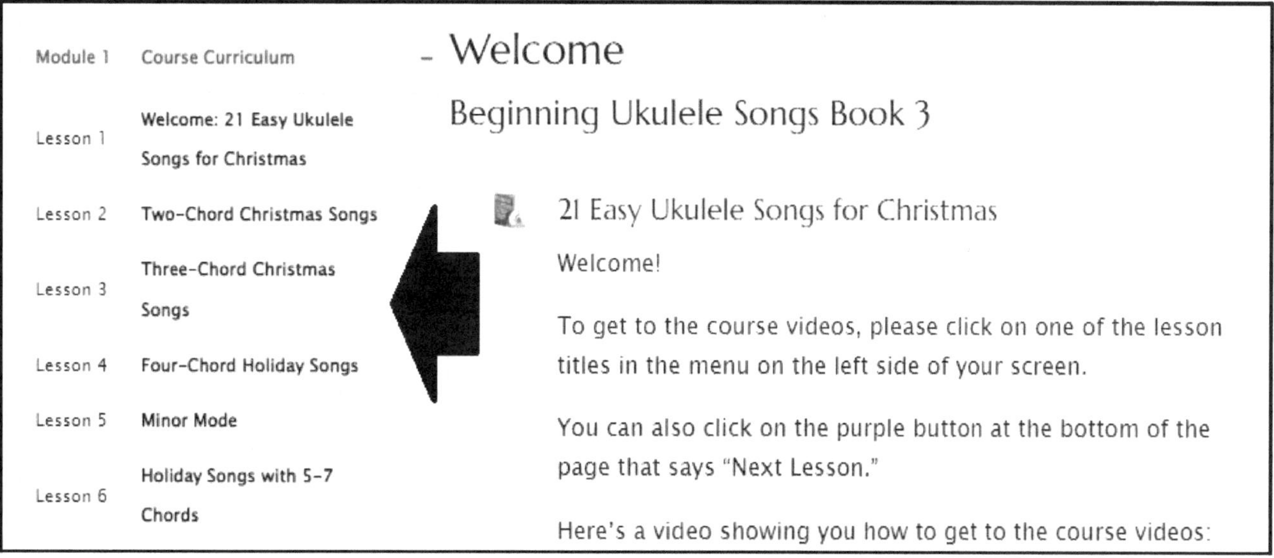

Get the Rest of the Beginning Ukulele Songs Series!

One of our books can help you move to the next level with your playing no matter where you are in your ukulele journey. All feature detailed and easy-to-follow instructions. We pick songs and carefully put them in an order that will help you build up gradually to more difficult skills. With our approach you'll continue to improve your playing without getting frustrated or developing bad habits.

Each is available in both paper and eBook versions and comes with its own companion video course at ukulele.io.

Book 1: 21 Songs in 6 Days: Learn Ukulele the Easy Way

Learn the five easiest ukulele chords (C, Am, F, C7, and G7) and three basic strums. Learn to change chords while keeping a steady strum going. By the end of the book, you'll be playing five chord songs. Book purchase includes a 101-minute video course to help you learn faster.

Get your copy at ukulele.io/Buy21Songs.

I could not have asked for a better way to learn the ukulele!! Pairing the book with the online video lessons was the perfect way for me to learn! I felt like I was having my own private lesson.

I can't wait to move onto the next book and keep learning! I have not been able to sing with my church choir nor ring in our bell choir, with everything that has happened. Music is cathartic for me and I am extremely thankful for my ukulele, which oddly enough I just had laying around, and for your books and videos. You have been a life saver!!

Thank you!!!

Daisy Richardson

Book 2: Easy Ukulele Songs: Five with Five Chords

Hone your ability to change chords by playing five favorite five chord songs. Learn four more easy chords. Learn fancier strumming patterns that combine the 3 basic strums from Book 1. Also get more practice with harder tab melodies and an introduction to the blues and blues improvisation in the key of C. Comes with a 10 video free course to help you learn the songs.

Get your copy at ukulele.io/5x5.

Total ukulele beginner. I enjoyed this work. It takes the skills learned in book 1 to a new level. I enjoyed a couple of the songs, especially "Five Foot Two." It's nice to find 1920s style songs because they are so naturally ukulele songs. I also enjoyed "Greensleeves" because the ukulele sounds more lute-like. The pedagogical learning approach is cool, thoughtful, and systematic. An excellent series. I bought this after reviewing other ukulele learning methods online and trying others from the library.

Book 3: 21 Easy Ukulele Songs for Christmas

21 seasonal favorites arranged in order of difficulty. After learning one new chord (D minor), you'll be able to play every song in the book with the chords you learned in Book 2 of the series. Get more practice reading tab melodies and using a variety of strumming patterns. The free course that comes with your book has a lesson video for every song in the book. Great for caroling or playing duets with fellow uke lovers.

Get your copy at ukulele.io/xmasnow.

I have purchased both the 21 songs in 6 days and the Christmas one. I have never picked up an Instrument in my 48 years of being on this earth and these books are making everything so easy to learn and are a lot of fun!!! THANK YOU!!!!!

You sure can use my name!

Scott Harkema

Book 4: 21 MORE Easy Ukulele Songs: Learn Intermediate Ukulele the Easy Way

Learn the most important intermediate ukulele chords, including the including the dreaded B flat chord: D, E minor, B flat, G minor, and C major 7.

You'll get more practice fingerpicking melodies and learn how to fingerpick accompaniments too. We'll introduce new fancier strumming patterns, songs in minor mode, and songs with three beats per measure. Also get more practice with the blues. Finally, you'll learn how to play great ukulele solo (chord melody) arrangements of several songs. All songs include both a standard music staff and tab notation, and several strumming patterns. The accompanying free course includes 40+ lesson videos.

Get your copy at ukulele.io/21MOREprint.

I thought you may like to know, I am joining my Ukulele group for a performance in a local village Hall, early in November. It may not be the greatest achievement ever, but I am looking forward to the show. Rest assured without the help of your books and videos, this experience would have been beyond me, thank you for helping have such fun.
Roy C. Edwards

Book 5: 21 Easy Ukulele Folk Songs

Learn 21 classic folk songs arranged in order of difficulty. The book begins with easy 2 chord songs and progresses to 7 chord songs in the key of G major. Lots of practice fingerpicking melodies and accompaniments and some great ukulele solo (chord melody) arrangements. Every song in the book has a lesson video, both standard music staff and tab notation and several strumming pattern suggestions. Includes favorites such as "Happy Birthday," "Take Me Out to the Ball Game," and "Shenandoah."

Get your copy at ukulele.io/folk.

This is the best formatted ukulele book that I have seen yet. I have bought many ukulele books and this series has taught me the most. This new Folk Song book is the best yet. Each song has a strumming pattern and tablature. Some of the songs are written with the chord melody, letting you play the chords and fingerpick at the same time. This was new to me, so beautiful, or will be soon.

Book 6: 21 Easy Ukulele Hymns

22 favorite hymns arranged in order of difficulty. The book begins with fourteen 2 and 3 chord hymns and includes favorites such as "Amazing Grace," "Be Thou My Vision," "Nearer My God to Thee" and "Fairest Lord Jesus." Many hymns are presented in 2 keys so you can choose a comfortable key for singing or playing. There's melody tab and a suggested strumming pattern for every hymn.

Get your copy at ukulele.io/hymns. The print copy does not include a free video course.

Check out our Hymn Kits at ukulele.io/hymnkits to get access to a 210-minute video course plus 13 chord melody hymn arrangements and bonus hymns.

I have been anxiously awaiting this book becoming available and it has been worth the wait. I received mine yesterday, and found myself going back to play songs out of it multiple times throughout the day. I love all the variety to the different ways to play the many songs-picking, strums, different keys. Playing these wonderful old hymns will bring hours of joy to my life, and I look forward to picking up extra tips from the video tutorials. I definitely would recommend adding this book to your ukulele music collection.
Janet Wentz

Other Courses That Work Great with Your Book

Do a deeper dive into various ukulele topics with our online courses and kits.

Learn Easy Ukulele Chord Melody Today!

Get everything you need to know to start playing chord melody at an easy level with this exciting course. If you can play the songs in our books, you can learn easy ukulele chord melody with this course. Find out more at ukulele.io/EasyChordMelody.

Learn to play chords and melody at the same time for a beautiful 'solo ukulele' sound.

Don't want to sing? This is the perfect course for you!

Easy Ukulele Hymn Kits

With a Hymn Kit you'll get:

a 45+ video course to help you learn the hymns.

sheet music for tags and turnarounds so you can connect your hymns together.

fabulous solo ukulele arrangements of hymns so you can play the melody and accompaniment yourself.

Available in Regular and Premium versions. Find out more at ukulele.io/21-easy-ukulele-hymns-is-here/.

Practice Makes Permanent

Do you want to learn how to practice better? Do you struggle with singing and strumming at the same time? Or, do you struggle with changing chords? Does fingerpicking sound cool, but it seems hard?

When you get our "Practice Makes Permanent Program," you learn how to practice. You make a deep dive into real improvement and a commitment to playing the ukulele well. You get an online membership that gives you weekly practice guidance. You improve on your ukulele. And you do it with a group of people who come together in a closed Facebook group.

You get:

- Practice charts and suggestions to organize your practicing
- Questions for reflection
- Membership in a closed Facebook Group to build community
- Periodic video updates that address questions from members

The program starts at the beginning of our first book, *21 Songs in 6 Days*, and moves through all 6 books. Along the way you learn the underlying musical skills of each song. You turbocharge your practice.

Learn more about this course at ukulele.io/permanent-program-basp-new/.

Chord Glossary

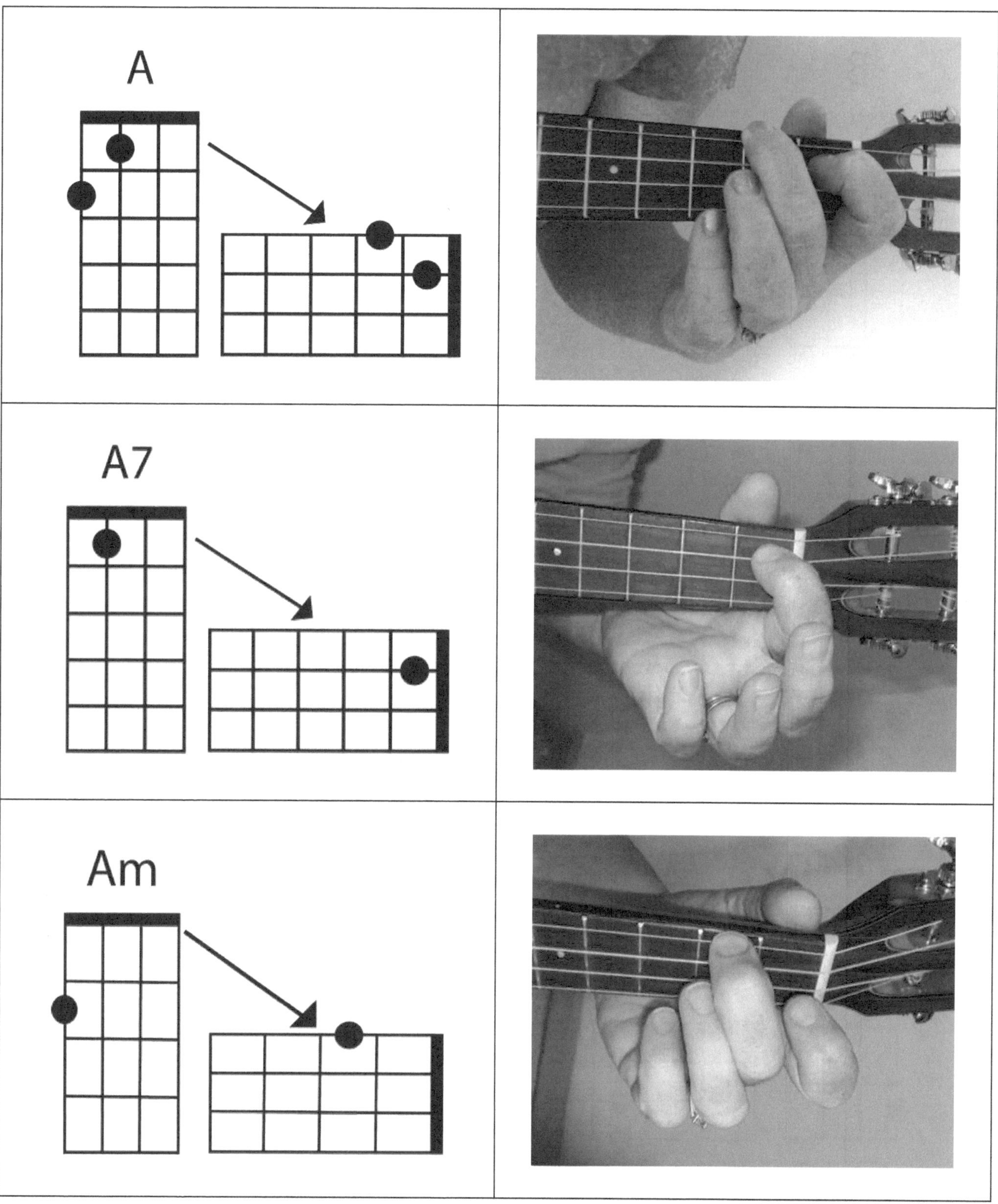

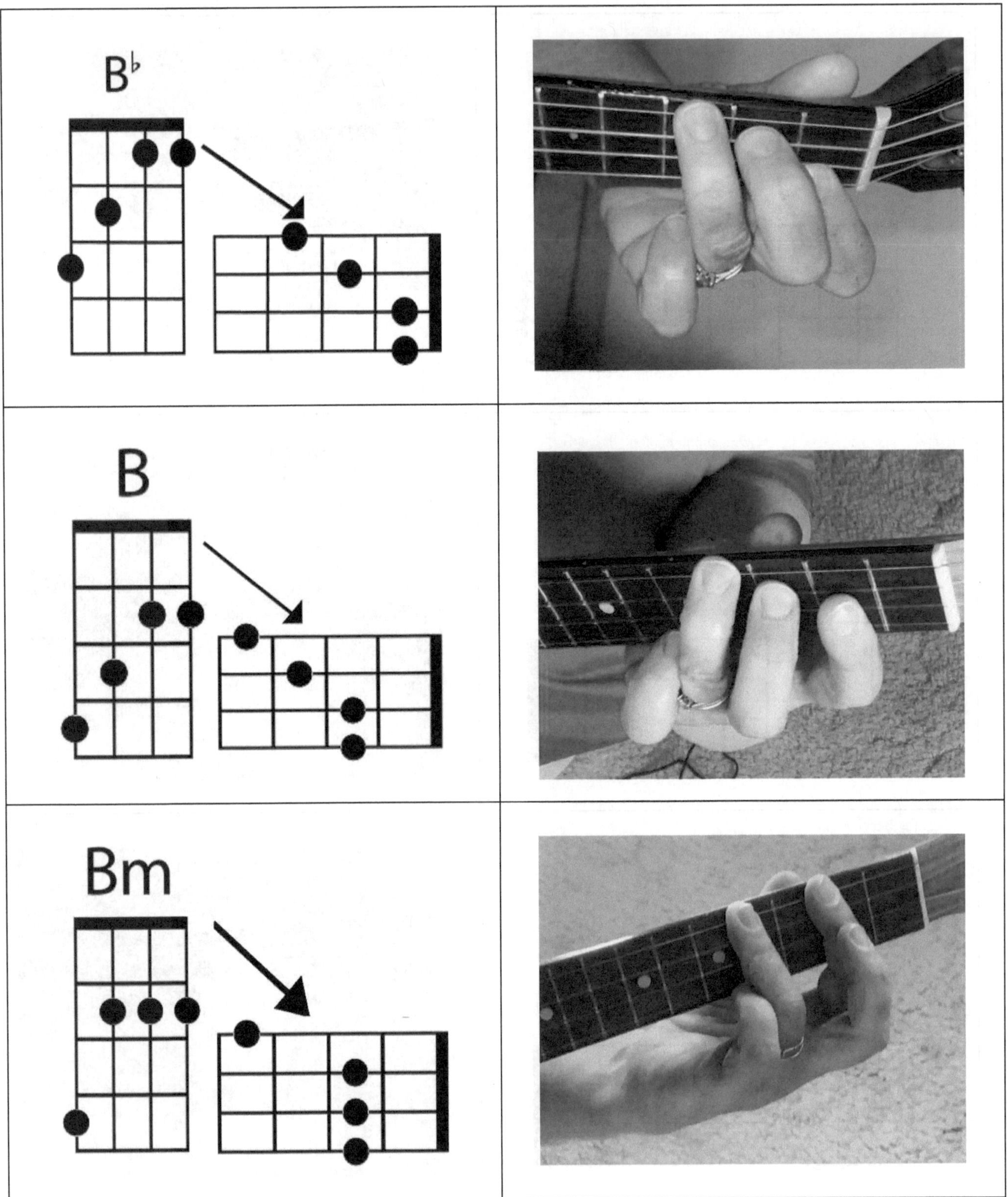
B♭
B
Bm

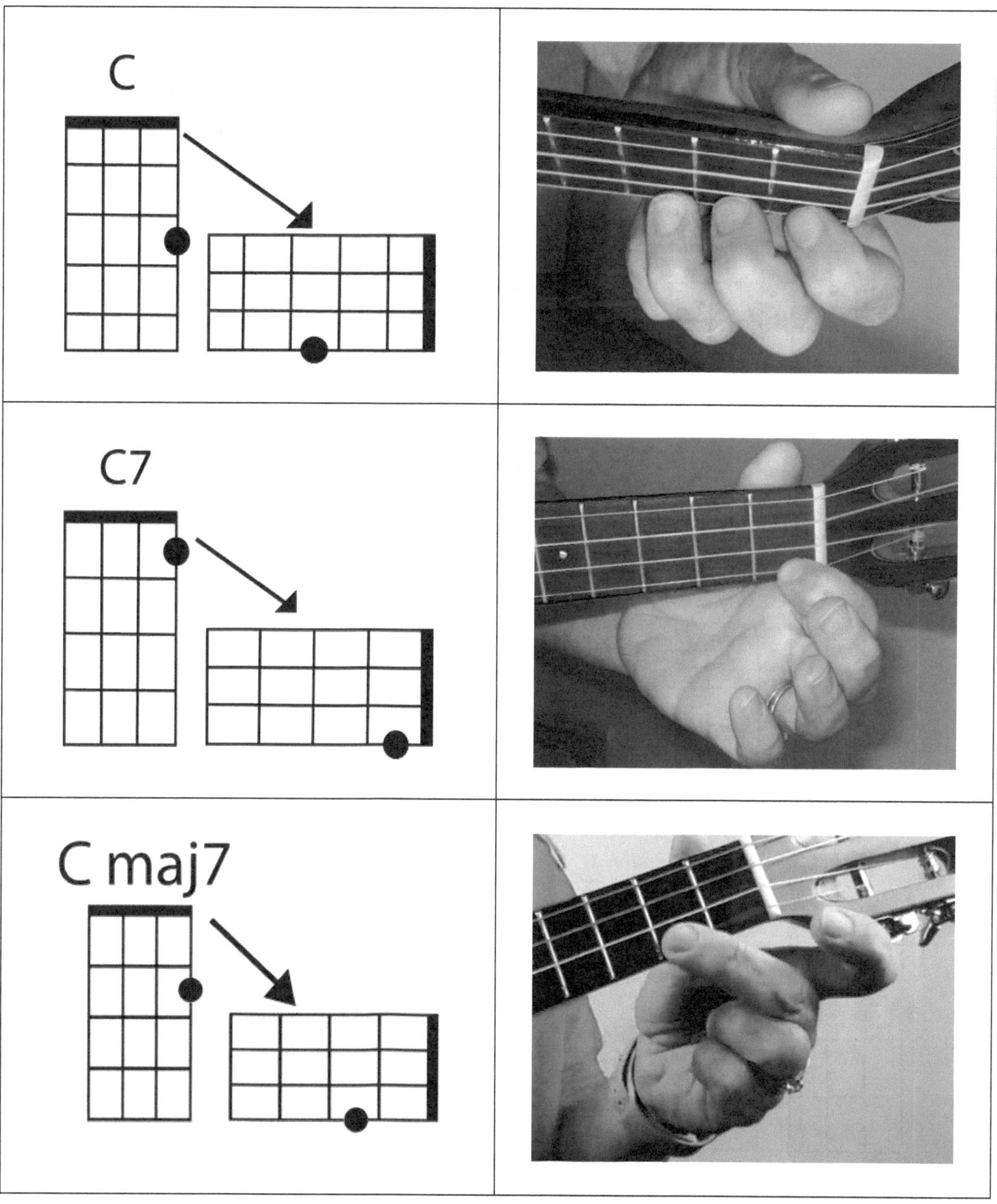
C
C7
C maj7

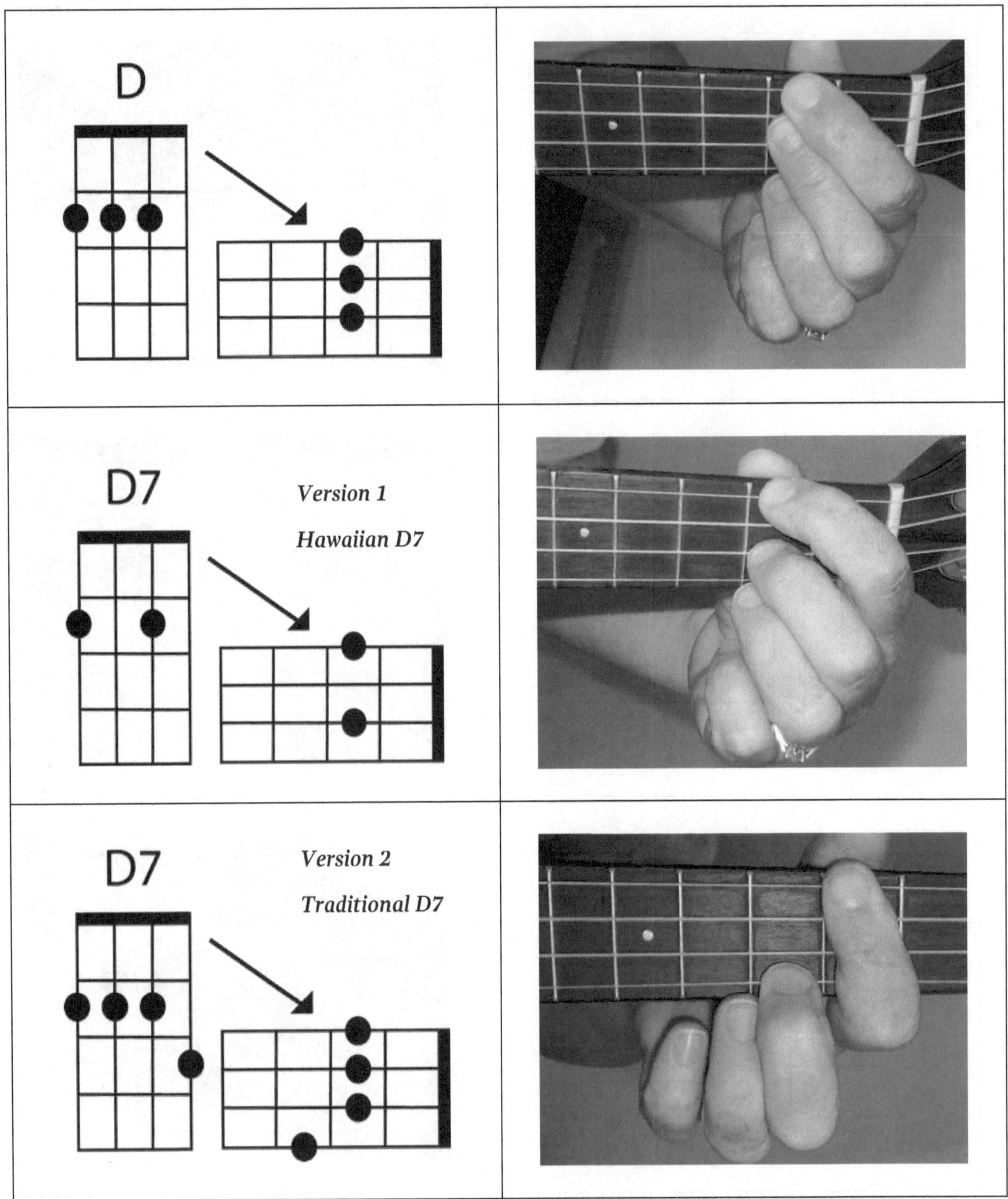
D
D7
Version 1
Hawaiian D7
D7
Version 2
Traditional D7

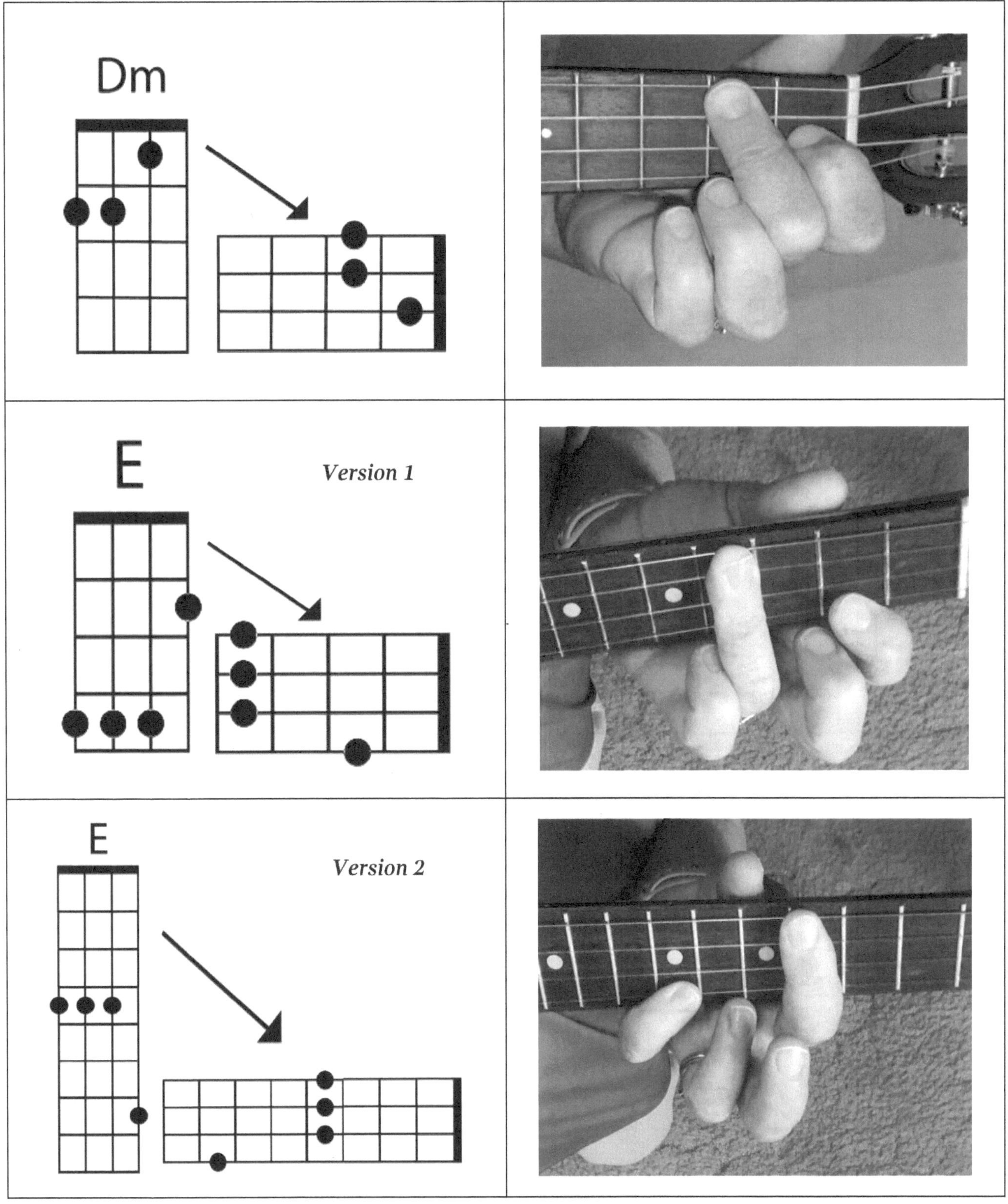
Dm
E
Version 1
E
Version 2

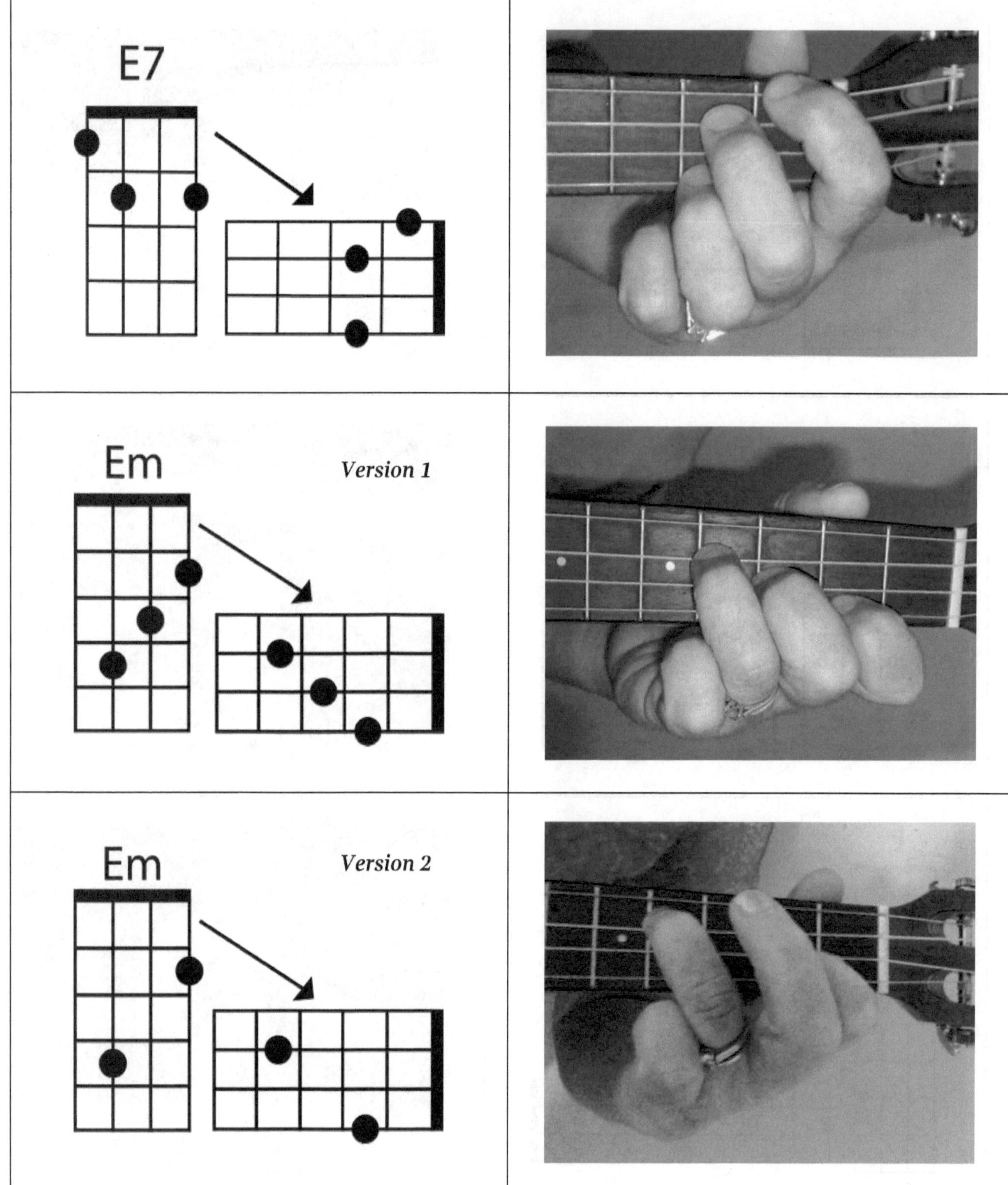
E7
Em
Version 1
Em
Version 2

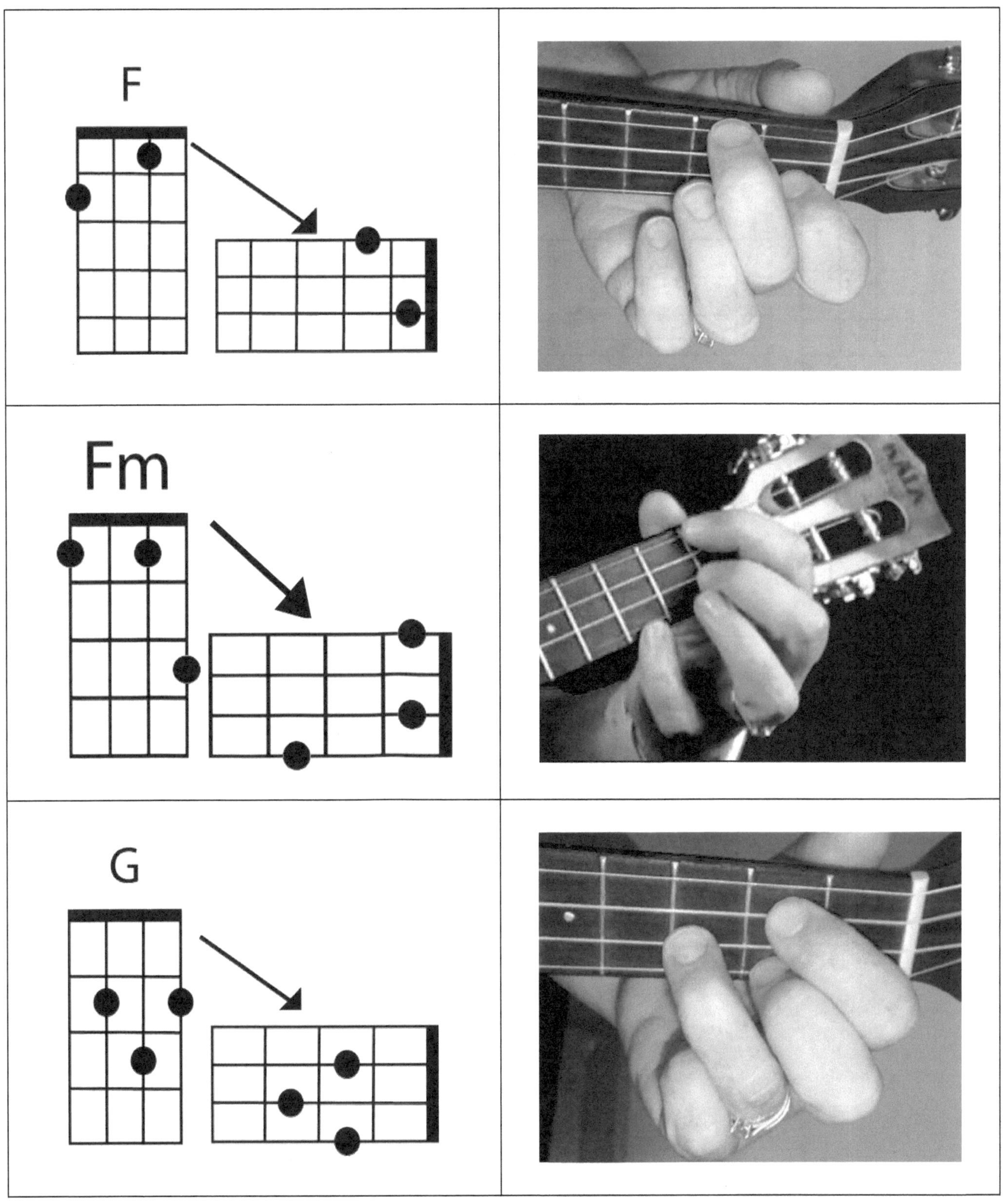
F
Fm
G
KALA

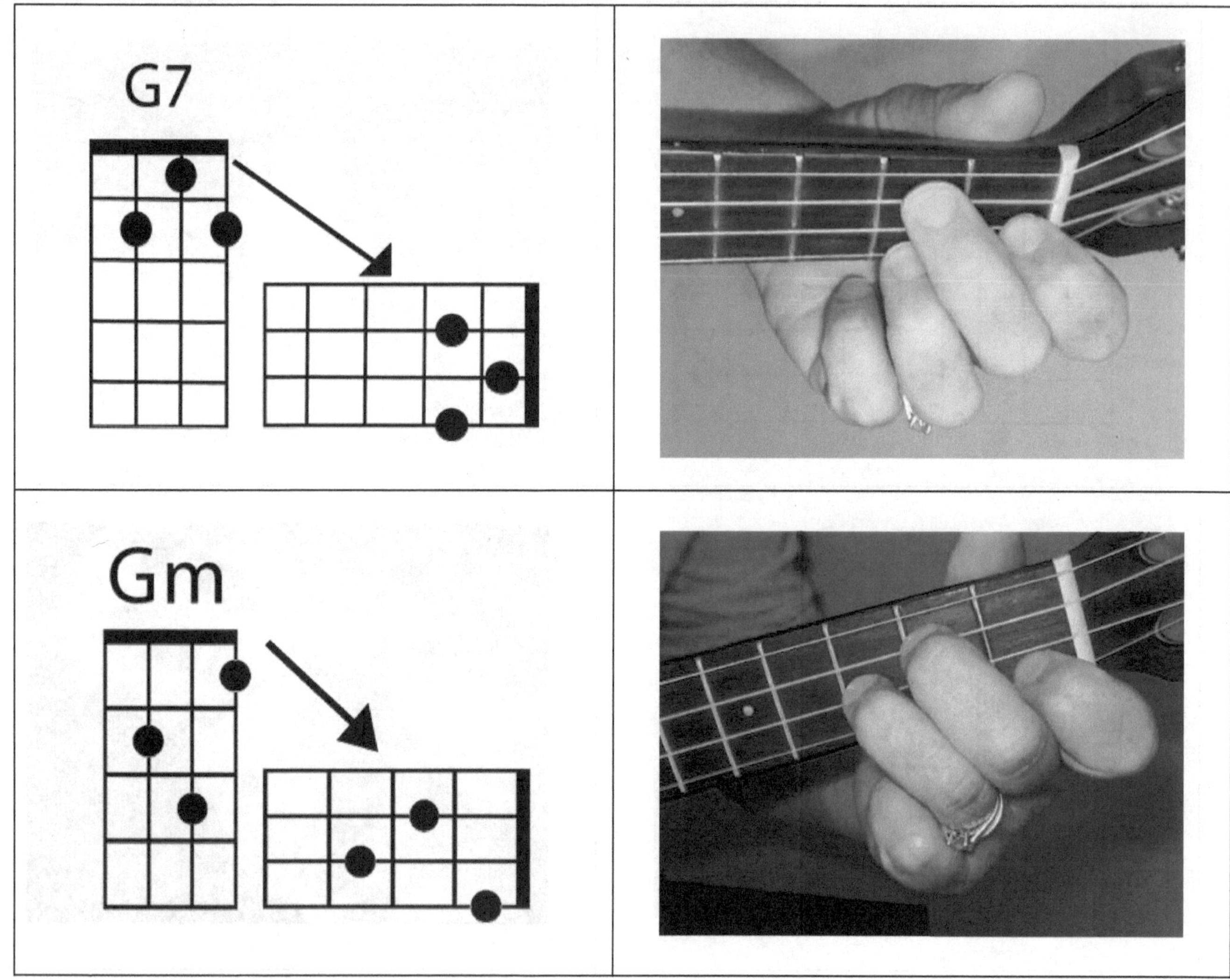
G7
Gm

About the Ukulele Sisters

Jenny Peters is a Grammy nominated full time music educator in the Chicago area. She has taught thousands of beginners on a variety of instruments during her many years of teaching.

Jenny developed her unique beginner-friendly method of teaching ukulele when she learned to play in order to include ukulele to her fourth grade General Music classes. She has gone on to become a popular YouTube ukulele personality who owns seven different kinds of ukuleles!

Jenny and Rebecca have now written six books in the Beginning Ukulele Songs series: Book 1, 21 Songs in 6 Days Learn Ukulele the Easy Way; Book 2, Easy Ukulele Songs: Five with Five Chords; Book 3, 21 Easy Ukulele Songs for Christmas; Book 4, 21 MORE Songs in 6 Days: Learn Intermediate Ukulele the Easy Way; Book 5, 21 Easy Ukulele Folk Songs, and Book 6, 21 Easy Ukulele Hymns.

The Illinois Music Educators Association has invited Jenny to do presentations on how to teach ukulele, and she has written articles on the subject for the magazine of the Illinois chapter of the American String Teachers Association. She is a member of the National Association for Music Education (NaFME), the American String Teachers Association (ASTA) and the American Society of Composers, Authors and Publishers (ASCAP). Jenny plays six other instruments besides ukulele: piano, violin, viola, cello, bass and organ. She currently heads a successful elementary and middle school orchestra program. Before that she taught Elementary General Music for ten years.

Jenny has served on the faculties of Lake Forest College and the College of Lake County. She taught piano, violin and chamber music at the Music Institute of Chicago and the Lake Forest Music Institute. She holds a Master of Music in Piano Performance from the University of Illinois and Bachelor of Music in Piano Performance from the University of Washington. She earned her teacher's certification from Trinity International University to share her passion for music with students of diverse backgrounds.

Rebecca Bogart has been introducing beginners of all ages to music for over 40 years. She believes that helping more people play music makes the world a better place.

She learned to play ukulele from her sister Jenny using the method taught in the Beginning Ukulele Songs series. While she has spent countless hours playing music with two hands at the piano, learning to have the left-hand fret chords while the right hand strummed was a surprisingly challenging experience! Rebecca brings a ukulele beginner's perspective to the Ukulele Sisters' writing team.

Rebecca has been passionate about the piano and music her entire life. She has played for audiences in Italy, taught master classes at Harvard and won more than a few piano competitions. She made her solo debut at Carnegie

Hall in early 2014. Several of Rebecca's piano students have won national and international awards and appeared on NPR's radio show "From the Top." She has been a featured presenter at the California Music Teachers Association and has recorded a CD of American solo piano music *American Retrospective.* She completed her Master's degree in Piano at the San Francisco Conservatory of Music.

Jenny Peters jenny@ukulele.io

Rebecca Bogart

facebook.com/UkuleleSisters/

youtube.com/c/Ukuleleio

instagram.com/jennypeters.theukulelesisters

Made in United States
Troutdale, OR
12/05/2024

25974292R00086